THE JEWISH CALENDAR

2015–2016

THE JEWISH MUSEUM NEW YORK – 5776

UNIVERSE

Published by UNIVERSE PUBLISHING
A Division of Rizzoli International Publications, Inc.
300 Park Avenue South
New York, NY 10010
www.rizzoliusa.com

Design by Hotfoot Studio
Printed in Hong Kong, PRC

Front cover:
Hanukkah Lamp
CandelabrAgam
Yaacov Agam (Israeli, b. 1928)
Israel, c. 1980
Copper alloy: cast; ball bearings
9¼ × 13¾ × 3⅞ in. (23.5 × 34.9 × 9.9 cm)
The Jewish Museum, New York
Gift of The Noon Foundation, Cecilia and Samuel Neaman, 1981-307a-j
Photo by Richard Goodbody, Inc.

Opposite page:
Alms Container
Moshe Zabari (Israeli, b. 1935)
New York, New York, United States, 1969
Silver: hammered and welded
4 × 3½ × 14 in. (10.2 × 8.9 × 35.6 cm)
The Jewish Museum, New York
Gift of the Albert A. List Family, JM 86-69
Photo by Richard Goodbody, Inc.

Back cover:
Torah Finial
Iran, 1946/47 (date of inscription)
Silver: pierced and engraved; paper: ink and gouache
10⅛ × 4¼ × 1¾ in. (25.7 × 10.8 × 4.4 cm)
The Jewish Museum, New York
Gift of Mena Rokhsar in memory of Ebrahim Khalil Rokhsar, 1993-238
Photo by John Parnell

August/September

Elul אלול

30 Sunday   15

31 Monday   16

Wall Hanging
Ottoman Palestine (Israel),
mid-19th–early 20th century
Perforated paper: embroidered with wool
18 × 23 in. (45.7 × 58.4 cm)
The Jewish Museum, New York
Gift of Dr. Harry G. Friedman, F 1260
Photo by John Parnell

Summer Bank Holiday (UK)

1 Tuesday   17

2 Wednesday   18

3 Thursday   19

4 Friday   20

5 Saturday   Parashat Ki Tavo / Selihot   21

AUGUST 2015

S	M	T	W	T	F	S
						1
2	3	4	5	6	7	8
9	10	11	12	13	14	15
16	17	18	19	20	21	22
23	24	25	26	27	28	29
30	31					

SEPTEMBER 2015

S	M	T	W	T	F	S
		1	2	3	4	5
6	7	8	9	10	11	12
13	14	15	16	17	18	19
20	21	22	23	24	25	26
27	28	29	30			

September

Elul אלול

6 Sunday   22

7 Monday   23

Torah Shield
Lublin (?) (Poland), 1838/39
(date of inscription)
Silver: repoussé, cast, engraved, and
parcel-gilt
8¹/₁₆ × 6¼ in. (20.5 × 15.9 cm)
The Jewish Museum, New York
Gift of the Danzig Jewish Community, D 125
Photo by John Parnell

Labor Day (US & Canada)

8 Tuesday   24

9 Wednesday   25

10 Thursday   26

SEPTEMBER 2015						
S	M	T	W	T	F	S
		1	2	3	4	5
6	7	8	9	10	11	12
13	14	15	16	17	18	19
20	21	22	23	24	25	26
27	28	29	30			

11 Friday   27

OCTOBER 2015						
S	M	T	W	T	F	S
				1	2	3
4	5	6	7	8	9	10
11	12	13	14	15	16	17
18	19	20	21	22	23	24
25	26	27	28	29	30	31

12 Saturday   Parashat Nitzavim   28

September

Elul/Tishri אלול/תשרי

13 Sunday — Erev Rosh ha-Shanah **29**

Rosh Hashanah
(Begins at Sundown)

14 Monday — Rosh ha-Shanah **1**

15 Tuesday — Rosh ha-Shanah **2**

16 Wednesday — Fast of Gedaliah **3**

17 Thursday **4**

18 Friday **5**

19 Saturday — Parashat Vayelekh / Shabbat Shuvah **6**

HELÈNE AYLON'S
Apple
Plate

FOR
CORTLAND
McINTOSH
GRANNY SMITH
AND
THAT OTHER KIND
OF APPLE

TO THE WOMAN HE SAID, THY HUSBAND SHALL BE THY DESIRE, BUT HE SHALL RULE OVER THEE.

September

Tishri תשרי

20 Sunday   7

Memorial Light
Bert Frijns (Dutch, b. 1953)
Landsmeer, Netherlands, 1987
Glass
25⁹⁄₁₆ × 11¹³⁄₁₆ in. (65 × 30 cm)
The Jewish Museum, New York
Purchase: Judaica Acquisitions Fund, 1990-18
Photo by John Parnell

21 Monday   8

International Day of Peace

22 Tuesday   Erev Yom Kippur   9

Yom Kippur (Begins at Sundown)

23 Wednesday   Yom Kippur   10
                  Yizkor

First Day of Autumn

24 Thursday   11

25 Friday   12

26 Saturday   Parashat Ha'azinu   13

September/October

Tishri תשרי

27 Sunday   Erev Sukkot **14**

Full Moon

28 Monday   First Day of Sukkot **15**

29 Tuesday   Second Day of Sukkot **16**

30 Wednesday   Hol ha-Mo'ed Sukkot **17**

1 Thursday   Hol ha-Mo'ed Sukkot **18**

2 Friday   Hol ha-Mo'ed Sukkot **19**

3 Saturday   Hol ha-Mo'ed Sukkot **20**

SEPTEMBER 2015

S	M	T	W	T	F	S
		1	2	3	4	5
6	7	8	9	10	11	12
13	14	15	16	17	18	19
20	21	22	23	24	25	26
27	28	29	30			

OCTOBER 2015

S	M	T	W	T	F	S
				1	2	3
4	5	6	7	8	9	10
11	12	13	14	15	16	17
18	19	20	21	22	23	24
25	26	27	28	29	30	31

October

Tishri תשרי

4	Sunday	Hoshana Rabba **21**
5	Monday	Shemini Atzeret Yizkor **22**
6	Tuesday	Simhat Torah **23**
7	Wednesday	**24**
8	Thursday	**25**
9	Friday	**26**
10	Saturday	Parashat Bereshit Shabbat Mevarekhim **27**

Torah Case
Tunisia, 1832
Wood: carved, gessoed, painted, and gilt
29⅛ × 18⅛ in. (74 × 46 cm)
The Jewish Museum, New York
Gift of Judge Mayer Sulzberger, S 508
Photo by John Parnell

OCTOBER 2015

S	M	T	W	T	F	S
				1	2	3
4	5	6	7	8	9	10
11	12	13	14	15	16	17
18	19	20	21	22	23	24
25	26	27	28	29	30	31

NOVEMBER 2015

S	M	T	W	T	F	S
1	2	3	4	5	6	7
8	9	10	11	12	13	14
15	16	17	18	19	20	21
22	23	24	25	26	27	28
29	30					

October

Tishri/Heshvan תשרי/חשון

11	Sunday	**28**

12	Monday	**29**

Columbus Day (US)
Thanksgiving Day (Canada)

13	Tuesday	Rosh Hodesh **30**

14	Wednesday	Rosh Hodesh **1**

15	Thursday	**2**

16	Friday	**3**

17	Saturday	Parashat No'ah **4**

Torah Pointer
Word
Brian Weissman (American, b. 1976)
Brooklyn, New York, United States, 2009
Silver: hand-worked with cast components
$12^{15}/_{16} \times 3^{5}/_{16} \times 1^{3}/_{4}$ in. (32.9 × 8.4 × 4.4 cm)
The Jewish Museum, New York
Purchase: Contemporary Judaica Acquisitions
Committee Fund, 2010-40
Photo by Richard Goodbody, Inc.

October

18 Sunday		5
19 Monday		6
20 Tuesday		7
21 Wednesday		8
22 Thursday		9
23 Friday		10
24 Saturday	Parashat Lekh Lekha	11

OCTOBER 2015

S	M	T	W	T	F	S
				1	2	3
4	5	6	7	8	9	10
11	12	13	14	15	16	17
18	19	20	21	22	23	24
25	26	27	28	29	30	31

NOVEMBER 2015

S	M	T	W	T	F	S
1	2	3	4	5	6	7
8	9	10	11	12	13	14
15	16	17	18	19	20	21
22	23	24	25	26	27	28
29	30					

October

Heshvan חשון

25 Sunday   **12**

26 Monday   **13**

Vase
Bezalel School
Jerusalem (Israel), c. 1920
Brass: inlaid with silver
$6^{7}/_{16} \times 3^{3}/_{8}$ in. (16.4 × 8.6 cm)
The Jewish Museum, New York
Gift of Dr. Harry G. Friedman, F 6106
Photo by Richard Goodbody, Inc.

27 Tuesday   **14**

Full Moon

28 Wednesday   **15**

29 Thursday   **16**

OCTOBER 2015

S	M	T	W	T	F	S
				1	2	3
4	5	6	7	8	9	10
11	12	13	14	15	16	17
18	19	20	21	22	23	24
25	26	27	28	29	30	31

30 Friday   **17**

NOVEMBER 2015

S	M	T	W	T	F	S
1	2	3	4	5	6	7
8	9	10	11	12	13	14
15	16	17	18	19	20	21
22	23	24	25	26	27	28
29	30					

31 Saturday   Parashat Vayera   **18**

Halloween

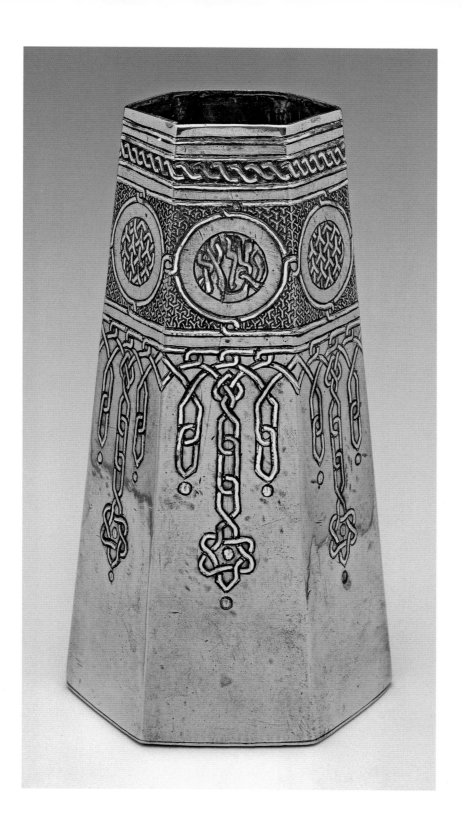

November

Heshvan חשון

1	Sunday	19

Daylight Saving Time Ends
(US & Canada)

2	Monday	20

3	Tuesday	21

Election Day (US)

4	Wednesday	22

5	Thursday	23

6	Friday	24

7	Saturday	Parashat Hayyei Sarah Shabbat Mevarekhim	25

Jug
Israel, 800–586 BCE
Clay: wheel-turned, slipped, fired, and wheel-burnished
10 9/16 × 6 7/16 in. (26.8 × 16.4 cm)
The Jewish Museum, New York
Gift of the Betty and Max Ratner Collection, 1981-154
Photo by Richard Goodbody, Inc.

November

Heshvan/Kislev חשון/כסלו

8 Sunday   26

Remembrance Sunday (UK)

9 Monday   27

10 Tuesday   28

11 Wednesday   29

Veterans Day (US)
Remembrance Day (Canada)

12 Thursday   Rosh Hodesh   30

13 Friday   Rosh Hodesh   1

14 Saturday   Parashat Toledot   2

NOVEMBER 2015

S	M	T	W	T	F	S
1	2	3	4	5	6	7
8	9	10	11	12	13	14
15	16	17	18	19	20	21
22	23	24	25	26	27	28
29	30					

DECEMBER 2015

S	M	T	W	T	F	S
		1	2	3	4	5
6	7	8	9	10	11	12
13	14	15	16	17	18	19
20	21	22	23	24	25	26
27	28	29	30	31		

November

Kislev כסלו

15 Sunday   3

16 Monday   4

Mezuzah Cover of Mas'uda Lakhriye
Morocco, 20th century
Silver: engraved and pierced
10¼ × 7 in. (26 × 17.8 cm)
The Jewish Museum, New York
Purchase: Judaica Acquisitions Fund,
1997-170
Photo by Richard Goodbody, Inc.

17 Tuesday   5

18 Wednesday   6

19 Thursday   7

NOVEMBER 2015

S	M	T	W	T	F	S
1	2	3	4	5	6	7
8	9	10	11	12	13	14
15	16	17	18	19	20	21
22	23	24	25	26	27	28
29	30					

20 Friday   8

DECEMBER 2015

S	M	T	W	T	F	S
		1	2	3	4	5
6	7	8	9	10	11	12
13	14	15	16	17	18	19
20	21	22	23	24	25	26
27	28	29	30	31		

21 Saturday   Parashat Vayeze   9

November   Kislev כסלו

22 Sunday   10

Tefillin Bag
Morocco or Tunisia, 1901
Silk velvet: embroidered with silk thread
11 × 9 in. (27.9 × 22.9 cm)
The Jewish Museum, New York
Gift of Dr. Harry G. Friedman, F 2902
Photo by John Parnell

23 Monday   11

24 Tuesday   12

25 Wednesday   13

Full Moon

26 Thursday   14

Thanksgiving Day (US)

27 Friday   15

28 Saturday   Parashat Vayishlah   16

November/December

29 Sunday   17

30 Monday   18

1 Tuesday   19

2 Wednesday   20

3 Thursday   21

4 Friday   22

5 Saturday   Parashat Vayeshev   23
                        Shabbat Mevarekhim

NOVEMBER 2015

S	M	T	W	T	F	S
1	2	3	4	5	6	7
8	9	10	11	12	13	14
15	16	17	18	19	20	21
22	23	24	25	26	27	28
29	30					

DECEMBER 2015

S	M	T	W	T	F	S
		1	2	3	4	5
6	7	8	9	10	11	12
13	14	15	16	17	18	19
20	21	22	23	24	25	26
27	28	29	30	31		

December

Kislev כסלו

6 Sunday · Erev Hanukkah **24**

Hanukkah (Begins at Sundown)

7 Monday · First Day of Hanukkah **25**

Hanukkah Lamp
David Heinz Gumbel
(Israeli, b. Germany 1896–1992)
Heilbronn, Germany, early 1930s
Silver: hand-worked
11⁹⁄₁₆ × 13⁵⁄₁₆ × 5¼ in.
(29.3 × 33.8 × 13.3 cm)
The Jewish Museum, New York
Gift of Hannah and Walter Flegenheimer,
2002-9a-d
Photo by Richard Goodbody, Inc.

8 Tuesday · Second Day of Hanukkah **26**

9 Wednesday · Third Day of Hanukkah **27**

10 Thursday · Fourth Day of Hanukkah **28**

Human Rights Day

11 Friday · Fifth Day of Hanukkah **29**

12 Saturday · Sixth Day of Hanukkah · Parashat Mi-kez · Rosh Hodesh **30**

DECEMBER 2015

S	M	T	W	T	F	S
		1	2	3	4	5
6	7	8	9	10	11	12
13	14	15	16	17	18	19
20	21	22	23	24	25	26
27	28	29	30	31		

JANUARY 2016

S	M	T	W	T	F	S
					1	2
3	4	5	6	7	8	9
10	11	12	13	14	15	16
17	18	19	20	21	22	23
24	25	26	27	28	29	30
31						

December

13	Sunday	Seventh Day of Hanukkah Rosh Hodesh	1

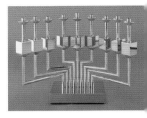

14	Monday	Eighth Day of Hanukkah	2

Hanukkah Lamp
CandelabrAgam
Yaacov Agam (Israeli, b. 1928)
Israel, c. 1980
Copper alloy: cast; ball bearings
9¼ × 13¾ × 3⅞ in.
(23.5 × 34.9 × 9.9 cm)
The Jewish Museum, New York
Gift of The Noon Foundation, Cecilia and
Samuel Neaman, 1981-307a-j
Photo by Richard Goodbody, Inc.

15	Tuesday		3

16	Wednesday		4

17	Thursday		5

18	Friday		6

19	Saturday	Parashat Vayiggash	7

December

20 Sunday   8

21 Monday   9

First Day of Winter

22 Tuesday   Fast of 10 Tevet   10

23 Wednesday   11

24 Thursday   12

25 Friday   13

Christmas

Full Moon

26 Saturday   Parashat Vayehi   14

Kwanzaa Begins

Boxing Day (Canada & UK)

DECEMBER 2015

S	M	T	W	T	F	S
		1	2	3	4	5
6	7	8	9	10	11	12
13	14	15	16	17	18	19
20	21	22	23	24	25	26
27	28	29	30	31		

JANUARY 2016

S	M	T	W	T	F	S
					1	2
3	4	5	6	7	8	9
10	11	12	13	14	15	16
17	18	19	20	21	22	23
24	25	26	27	28	29	30
31						

December 2015/January 2016   Tevet טבת

27 Sunday   **15**

28 Monday   **16**

Rug depicting Theodor Herzl
Alliance Israelite Universelle School
Jerusalem (Israel), c. 1900
Machine pile weave rug
44 × 25¼ in. (111.8 × 64.1 cm)
The Jewish Museum, New York
Gift of the Solomon Family, New York City, 1995-83
Photo by John Parnell

29 Tuesday   **17**

30 Wednesday   **18**

31 Thursday   **19**

DECEMBER 2015						
S	M	T	W	T	F	S
		1	2	3	4	5
6	7	8	9	10	11	12
13	14	15	16	17	18	19
20	21	22	23	24	25	26
27	28	29	30	31		

1 Friday   **20**

New Year's Day

2 Saturday   Parashat Shemot   **21**

JANUARY 2016						
S	M	T	W	T	F	S
					1	2
3	4	5	6	7	8	9
10	11	12	13	14	15	16
17	18	19	20	21	22	23
24	25	26	27	28	29	30
31						

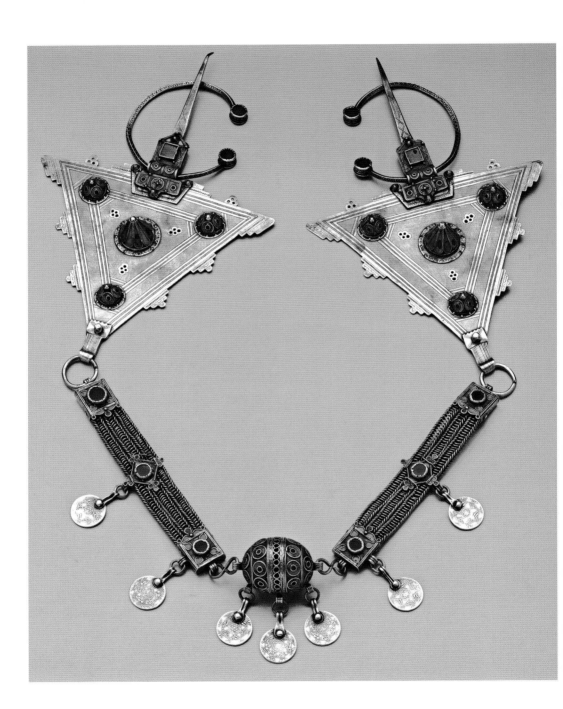

January

Tevet טבת

| 3 | Sunday | 22 |

| 4 | Monday | 23 |

| 5 | Tuesday | 24 |

| 6 | Wednesday | 25 |

| 7 | Thursday | 26 |

JANUARY

S	M	T	W	T	F	S
					1	2
3	4	5	6	7	8	9
10	11	12	13	14	15	16
17	18	19	20	21	22	23
24	25	26	27	28	29	30
31						

| 8 | Friday | 27 |

FEBRUARY

S	M	T	W	T	F	S
	1	2	3	4	5	6
7	8	9	10	11	12	13
14	15	16	17	18	19	20
21	22	23	24	25	26	27
28	29					

| 9 | Saturday | Parashat Va-era / Shabbat Mevarekhim | 28 |

January

Tevet/Shevat טבת/שבט

10 Sunday		29

11 Monday	Rosh Hodesh	1

Spice Container
Iris Tutnauer (Israeli, b. 1964)
Jerusalem, Israel, 1998
Silver
2 × 6⅝ × 2 in. (5.1 × 16.8 × 5.1 cm)
The Jewish Museum, New York
Purchase: The Hyman and Miriam Silver
Fund for Contemporary Judaica, 2001-21
Photo by Richard Goodbody, Inc.

12 Tuesday	2

13 Wednesday	3

14 Thursday	4

15 Friday	5

16 Saturday	Parashat Bo	6

January

Shevat שבט

17 Sunday   7

18 Monday   8

Martin Luther King Jr. Day (US)

19 Tuesday   9

20 Wednesday   10

21 Thursday   11

22 Friday   12

23 Saturday   Parashat Be-Shallah   13
                       Shabbat Shirah

Full Moon

January

Shevat שבט

24 Sunday   14

25 Monday   Tu Bishvat   15

Torah Crown (?)
Munich (Germany), c. 1725–50
Silver: repoussé, pierced, and parcel-gilt; glass
6¹⁵⁄₁₆ × 6⁷⁄₈ in. (17.7 × 17.5 cm)
The Jewish Museum, New York
Gift of Dr. Harry G. Friedman, F 1749
Photo by John Parnell

26 Tuesday   16

27 Wednesday   17

28 Thursday   18

JANUARY						
S	M	T	W	T	F	S
					1	2
3	4	5	6	7	8	9
10	11	12	13	14	15	16
17	18	19	20	21	22	23
24	25	26	27	28	29	30
31						

29 Friday   19

FEBRUARY						
S	M	T	W	T	F	S
	1	2	3	4	5	6
7	8	9	10	11	12	13
14	15	16	17	18	19	20
21	22	23	24	25	26	27
28	29					

30 Saturday   Parashat Yitro   20

January/February

Shevat שבט

31 Sunday   21

1 Monday   22

Cooking Pot
Frankfurt am Main (Germany), 1579/80
(date of inscription)
Brass: cast, chased, and hammered
8 × 12 × 9 in. (20.3 × 30.5 × 22.9 cm)
The Jewish Museum, New York
Gift of Mr. and Mrs. Ben Heller, JM 23-64
Photo by John Parnell

2 Tuesday   23

Groundhog Day

3 Wednesday   24

4 Thursday   25

5 Friday   26

6 Saturday   Parashat Mishpatim   **27**
                    Shabbat Mevarekhim

February

7   Sunday   **28**

8   Monday   **29**

Chinese New Year

9   Tuesday   Rosh Hodesh   **30**

10   Wednesday   Rosh Hodesh   **1**

Ash Wednesday

11   Thursday   **2**

12   Friday   **3**

13   Saturday   Parashat Terumah   **4**

FEBRUARY

S	M	T	W	T	F	S
		1	2	3	4	5	6
7	8	9	10	11	12	13
14	15	16	17	18	19	20
21	22	23	24	25	26	27
28	29					

MARCH

S	M	T	W	T	F	S
		1	2	3	4	5
6	7	8	9	10	11	12
13	14	15	16	17	18	19
20	21	22	23	24	25	26
27	28	29	30	31		

February

Adar I אדר א'

14 Sunday   **5**

St. Valentine's Day

15 Monday   **6**

Hallah Cover
Afghanistan (?), 1970s
Synthetic fabric and cotton: machine stitched
28 × 30 in. (71.1 × 76.2 cm)
The Jewish Museum, New York
Gift of Liza Kashi-Basal, 1998-51
Photo by John Parnell

Presidents' Day (US)

16 Tuesday   **7**

17 Wednesday   **8**

18 Thursday   **9**

FEBRUARY						
S	M	T	W	T	F	S
	1	2	3	4	5	6
7	8	9	10	11	12	13
14	15	16	17	18	19	20
21	22	23	24	25	26	27
28	29					

19 Friday   **10**

MARCH						
S	M	T	W	T	F	S
		1	2	3	4	5
6	7	8	9	10	11	12
13	14	15	16	17	18	19
20	21	22	23	24	25	26
27	28	29	30	31		

20 Saturday   Parashat Tezavveh   **11**

February

21	Sunday	**12**

22	Monday	**13**

Full Moon

23	Tuesday	**14**

24	Wednesday	**15**

25	Thursday	**16**

26	Friday	**17**

27	Saturday	Parashat Ki Tissa **18**

Horse Figurine
Israel, 1000–586 BCE
Clay: hand-formed, incised, and fired
3¹⁵⁄₁₆ × 1⁵⁄₁₆ × 5¹⁵⁄₁₆ in.
(10 × 3.3 × 15.1 cm)
The Jewish Museum, New York
Gift of the Betty and Max Ratner
Collection, 1981-223
Photo by Ardon Bar Hama

February/March

28 Sunday   **19**

29 Monday   **20**

1 Tuesday   **21**

2 Wednesday   **22**

3 Thursday   **23**

FEBRUARY

S	M	T	W	T	F	S
	1	2	3	4	5	6
7	8	9	10	11	12	13
14	15	16	17	18	19	20
21	22	23	24	25	26	27
28	29					

4 Friday   **24**

MARCH

S	M	T	W	T	F	S
		1	2	3	4	5
6	7	8	9	10	11	12
13	14	15	16	17	18	19
20	21	22	23	24	25	26
27	28	29	30	31		

5 Saturday   Parashat Vayakhel / Shabbat Shekalim / Shabbat Mevarekhim   **25**

March

6   Sunday   26

7   Monday   27

Multipurpose Cube
Zelig Segal (Israeli, b. 1933)
Israel, 1986
Aluminum: milled
$3^{15}/_{16} \times 3^{15}/_{16} \times 3^{15}/_{16}$ in.
($10 \times 10 \times 10$ cm)
The Jewish Museum, New York
Gift of Marcia Riklis, 1999-6
Photo by Richard Goodbody, Inc.

8   Tuesday   28

International Women's Day

9   Wednesday   29

10   Thursday   Rosh Hodesh   30

11   Friday   Rosh Hodesh   1

12   Saturday   Parashat Pekudei   2

			FEBRUARY			
S	M	T	W	T	F	S
		1	2	3	4	5	6
7	8	9	10	11	12	13
14	15	16	17	18	19	20
21	22	23	24	25	26	27
28	29					

			MARCH			
S	M	T	W	T	F	S
		1	2	3	4	5
6	7	8	9	10	11	12
13	14	15	16	17	18	19
20	21	22	23	24	25	26
27	28	29	30	31		

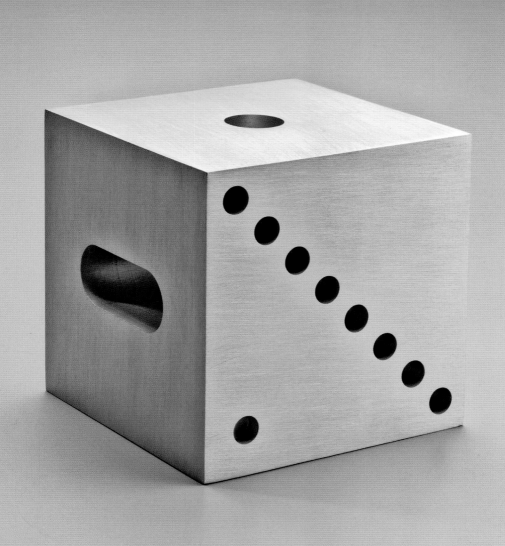

March

Adar II אדר ב׳

13 Sunday   3

Daylight Saving Time Begins
(US & Canada)

14 Monday   4

Purim Gift Bags
British Mandate Palestine (Israel),
before 1948
Cotton twill: block printed
Each: 7½ × 5¼ in. (19.1 × 13.3 cm)
The Jewish Museum, New York
Gift of Dr. Alexander Marx, S 1044a-i
Photo by Richard Goodbody, Inc.

15 Tuesday   5

16 Wednesday   6

17 Thursday   7

St. Patrick's Day

18 Friday   8

19 Saturday   Parashat Vayikra   9
Shabbat Zakhor

March

Adar II אדר ב׳

20 Sunday   10

First Day of Spring
Palm Sunday

21 Monday   11

22 Tuesday   12

23 Wednesday   Fast of Esther   13
                                      Erev Purim

Full Moon

24 Thursday   Purim   14

25 Friday   Shushan Purim 15

Good Friday

26 Saturday   Parashat Zav   16

March/April

27 Sunday   17

Easter
---

28 Monday   18

Torah Finials
Heinrich Wilhelm Kompff
(active 1783–1825)
Kassel (Germany), 1797–99
Silver: engraved
Each: 11 × 3¾ in. (27.9 × 9.5 cm)
The Jewish Museum, New York
Purchase: Gift of Dr. Harry G. Friedman,
by exchange; Judaica Acquisitions Fund;
and Frances and Hubert J. Brandt Gift,
1999-107a-b
Photo by Richard Goodbody, Inc.

Easter Monday (Canada & UK)
---

29 Tuesday   19

30 Wednesday   20

31 Thursday   21

MARCH

S	M	T	W	T	F	S
		1	2	3	4	5
6	7	8	9	10	11	12
13	14	15	16	17	18	19
20	21	22	23	24	25	26
27	28	29	30	31		

1 Friday   22

APRIL

S	M	T	W	T	F	S
					1	2
3	4	5	6	7	8	9
10	11	12	13	14	15	16
17	18	19	20	21	22	23
24	25	26	27	28	29	30

2 Saturday   Parshat Shemini   23
Shabbat Parah
Shabbat Mevarekhim

April

Adar II/Nisan אדר ב׳/ניסן

3   Sunday   24

4   Monday   25

call Elaine 15m re interviews from add call Jackie re mtg + move & concern re letter to C. Review photos/ink Costco.

5   Tuesday   26

6   Wednesday   27

7   Thursday *re mail re Exect. coverage.*   28

8   Friday   29

9   Saturday   Parashat Tazria   1
                   Rosh Hodesh
           Shabbat Ha-Hodesh

Cup
Eastern Mediterranean, 3rd century CE
Glass: free-blown and wheel-ground
3 9/16 × 3 1/8 in. (9 × 7.9 cm)
The Jewish Museum, New York
Gift of Elaine and Harvey Rothenberg,
JM 98-79
Photo by Ardon Bar Hama

April

Nisan ניסן

10 Sunday   2

11 Monday   3

12 Tuesday   4

Jackie re "Tardy"

13 Wednesday   5

Maurice ... AGM.

		APRIL				
S	M	T	W	T	F	S
					1	2
3	4	5	6	7	8	9
10	11	12	13	14	15	16
17	18	19	20	21	22	23
24	25	26	27	28	29	30

14 Thursday   6

Lorrie - re AGM

		MAY				
S	M	T	W	T	F	S
1	2	3	4	5	6	7
8	9	10	11	12	13	14
15	16	17	18	19	20	21
22	23	24	25	26	27	28
29	30	31				

15 Friday   7

16 Saturday   Parashat Mezora   8
                                                    Shabbat Hagadol

April

17 Sunday   9

18 Monday   10

Miriam Cup

Amy Klein Reichert (American, b. 1959)

Manufacturer: Stephen Smithers (American, b. 1951)

Williamstown, Massachusetts, United States, 1997

Silver: cast and hammered

4½ × 7¾ in. (11.4 × 19.7 cm)

The Jewish Museum, New York

Purchase: Lorraine and Martin Beitler Foundation Gift and Judaica Acquisitions Fund, 1997-131

Photo by Richard Goodbody, Inc.

19 Tuesday   11

20 Wednesday   12

21 Thursday   13

S	M	T	W	T	F	S
					1	2
3	4	5	6	7	8	9
10	11	12	13	14	15	16
17	18	19	20	21	22	23
24	25	26	27	28	29	30

22 Friday   Erev Pesah   14

Passover (Begins at Sundown)

Full Moon

Earth Day

MAY

S	M	T	W	T	F	S
1	2	3	4	5	6	7
8	9	10	11	12	13	14
15	16	17	18	19	20	21
22	23	24	25	26	27	28
29	30	31				

23 Saturday   First Day of Pesah   15

April

Nisan ניסן

24 Sunday

Second Day of Pesah
Sefirat ha-Omer begins **16**

---

25 Monday

Hol ha-Mo-ed Pesah **17**

---

26 Tuesday

Hol ha-Mo-ed Pesah **18**

---

27 Wednesday

Hol ha-Mo-ed Pesah **19**

---

28 Thursday

Hol ha-Mo-ed Pesah **20**

---

29 Friday

Seventh Day of Pesah **21**

---

30 Saturday

Eighth Day of Pesah
Yizkor **22**

Matzah Bag
S N
Europe, 19th century
Silk: embroidered with silk thread;
glass beads; cotton
15¹⁵⁄₁₆ × 15³⁄₁₆ in. (40.5 × 38.5 cm)
The Jewish Museum, New York
Gift of Mr. and Mrs. Max Gottschalk,
JM 47-59
Photo by Malcom Varon

APRIL

S	M	T	W	T	F	S
					1	2
3	4	5	6	7	8	9
10	11	12	13	14	15	16
17	18	19	20	21	22	23
24	25	26	27	28	29	30

MAY

S	M	T	W	T	F	S
1	2	3	4	5	6	7
8	9	10	11	12	13	14
15	16	17	18	19	20	21
22	23	24	25	26	27	28
29	30	31				

May

Nisan ניסן

1   Sunday   23

Orthodox Easter

2   Monday   24

Robe
Djoma
Samarkand (Uzbekistan), late 19th centu
Silk: ikat; cotton: printed
55 in. (139.7 cm)
The Jewish Museum, New York
Gift of Ben Zion Aron Bayof in memory
of his father Rachamim ben Shalomo
Aron-Bayof and his wife's father Yonah
Niez Bayof, JM 216-68
Photo by John Parnell

Early May Bank Holiday (UK)

3   Tuesday   25

4   Wednesday   26

5   Thursday   Yom ha-Sho'ah   27

6   Friday   28

7   Saturday   Parashat Aharei Mot   29
                  Shabbat Mevarekhim

May

Nisan/Iyyar ניסן/אייר

8 Sunday

Rosh Hodesh **30**

Mother's Day

9 Monday

Rosh Hodesh **1**

10 Tuesday

2

11 Wednesday

Yom ha-Zikkaron **3**

12 Thursday

Yom ha-Azma'ut **4**

13 Friday

5

14 Saturday

Parashat Kedoshim **6**

MAY

S	M	T	W	T	F	S
1	2	3	4	5	6	7
8	9	10	11	12	13	14
15	16	17	18	19	20	21
22	23	24	25	26	27	28
29	30	31				

JUNE

S	M	T	W	T	F	S
			1	2	3	4
5	6	7	8	9	10	11
12	13	14	15	16	17	18
19	20	21	22	23	24	25
26	27	28	29	30		

May

Iyyar אייר

15 Sunday   7

16 Monday   8

Torah Shield
Johann Ziehrer (b. 1844;
active 1878–1913)
Vienna (Austria), 1878–1908
Silver: repoussé, chased, and parcel-gilt
11⁹⁄₁₆ × 10¾ in. (29.3 × 27.3 cm)
The Jewish Museum, New York
Gift of Dr. Harry G. Friedman, F 245
Photo by John Parnell

17 Tuesday   9

18 Wednesday   10

19 Thursday   11

MAY						
S	M	T	W	T	F	S
1	2	3	4	5	6	7
8	9	10	11	12	13	14
15	16	17	18	19	20	21
22	23	24	25	26	27	28
29	30	31				

20 Friday   12

JUNE						
S	M	T	W	T	F	S
			1	2	3	4
5	6	7	8	9	10	11
12	13	14	15	16	17	18
19	20	21	22	23	24	25
26	27	28	29	30		

21 Saturday   Parashat Emor   13

Full Moon

May

Iyyar אייר

22 Sunday   **14**

23 Monday   **15**

Marriage Contract
Verona (Italy), 1733
Ink and paint on parchment
29½ × 19½ in. (74.9 × 49.5 cm)
The Jewish Museum, New York
Gift of Isidore M. Cohen, JM 81-76
Photo by Ardon Bar Hama

Victoria Day (Canada)

24 Tuesday   **16**

25 Wednesday   **17**

26 Thursday   Lag ba-Omer   **18**

27 Friday   **19**

28 Saturday   Parashat Behar   **20**

MAY

S	M	T	W	T	F	S
1	2	3	4	5	6	7
8	9	10	11	12	13	14
15	16	17	18	19	20	21
22	23	24	25	26	27	28
29	30	31				

JUNE

S	M	T	W	T	F	S
			1	2	3	4
5	6	7	8	9	10	11
12	13	14	15	16	17	18
19	20	21	22	23	24	25
26	27	28	29	30		

בסימנא טבא

בחמישי בשבת שני ימים לחדש אייר שנת חמשת אלפים וארבע מאות ותשעים
ושלש לבריאת עולם למנין שאנו מנין פה קק ווירונא היכי כ שמואל בן חמנה כ משול
אקן לל אמר לה לחרא מרתבא לאה בת חמנה כ מנחם מאישטילה זל דהיולי לאנתו כדת משה
וישראל ואנא אפלח ואיקיר און ואפרנט יתי כהלכת עברין יהודאי דפלחין ומיקרין וזני
ומפרנסין ית נשדהון בקושטא ויהיבנא ליכי מוהר מרתרכבא כסף זוזי מאה דחזי ליכי מדאוריתא
וכסותיכי וספוקיכי ומיעל לותיכי כארח כל ארעא וצביאת מרתבא חבגרה מרת לאה מת מתרכתא
דא והות ליה לאנתו דא נדוניא רגעלתא ליה אלף חמיש מאות דייבאסי ליעך ששוה טדריו
וארבעה מרקיני לאהר מסכין קרינט פה ווירונא בל קך מיעה מרושבש דעוד בע בע מאות
דמפטאר כ שמואל ...

אראריות וחומי שטר כתובה ...

May/June

Iyyar אייר

29 Sunday   21

30 Monday   22

Memorial Day (US)
Spring Bank Holiday (UK)

31 Tuesday   23

1 Wednesday   24

2 Thursday   25

3 Friday   26

4 Saturday   Parashat Behukkotai   **27**
               Shabbat Mevarekhim

Prayer Shawl Bag
Çanakkale, Ottoman Empire (Turkey),
second half 19th century
Woven silk with metallic thread;
mother-of-pearl button
9⅛ × 10⁷/₁₆ in. (23.2 × 26.5 cm)
The Jewish Museum, New York
Gift of Bessie Franco, 1986-123
Photo by Joseph Sachs

June

5 Sunday   Yom Yerushalayim **28**

6 Monday   **29**

Tina – 10min –

7 Tuesday   Rosh Hodesh **1**

Aloma – 20min –

8 Wednesday   **2**

9 Thursday   **3**

Aloma – 4pm – hr – 11am

10 Friday   **4**

11 Saturday   Parashat Bemidbar / Erev Shavuot **5**

MAY

S	M	T	W	T	F	S
1	2	3	4	5	6	7
8	9	10	11	12	13	14
15	16	17	18	19	20	21
22	23	24	25	26	27	28
29	30	31				

JUNE

S	M	T	W	T	F	S
			1	2	3	4
5	6	7	8	9	10	11
12	13	14	15	16	17	18
19	20	21	22	23	24	25
26	27	28	29	30		

June

Sivan סיון

12 Sunday · Shavuot **6**

13 Monday · Shavuot · Yizkor **7**

Torah Crown
Europe, late 19th–early 20th century
Brass: die-stamped, pierced, chased, engraved; traces of silver-plating
6⅜ × 5⅝ in. (16.2 × 14.3 cm)
The Jewish Museum, New York
Gift of the Danzig Jewish Community, D 56
Photo by John Parnell

14 Tuesday **8**

15 Wednesday **9**

16 Thursday **10**

17 Friday · *call Aloma.* **11**

18 Saturday · *print out the "New Soc:* · Parashat Naso **12**
look up - read, print "Act"

June

Sivan סיון

19 Sunday

13

call Jackie —

Father's Day

20 Monday

14

call from Amy
call from Mlenra re AGM

First Day of Summer
Full Moon

21 Tuesday

15

AGM 37km

22 Wednesday

16

call from ... concerns —
call J

23 Thursday

17

Email — exec meeting / Bonnie
Greg/Ann

24 Friday

18

c — Alome
Email Alome re Sche — x Til
*   "   "   " Hgt minutes —*

25 Saturday

Parashat Beha'alotekha

19

Unknown Artist/Maker
***Presentation Drawing for the
Interior of a Synagogue,*** **c. 1910**
Watercolor and graphite on paper
10⅛ × 13½ in. (25.7 × 34.3 cm)
The Jewish Museum, New York
Gift of Elaine Lustig Cohen in memory
of Arthur A. Cohen, 1989-1
Photo by John Parnell

JUNE						
S	M	T	W	T	F	S
			1	2	3	4
5	6	7	8	9	10	11
12	13	14	15	16	17	18
19	20	21	22	23	24	25
26	27	28	29	30		

JULY						
S	M	T	W	T	F	S
					1	2
3	4	5	6	7	8	9
10	11	12	13	14	15	16
17	18	19	20	21	22	23
24	25	26	27	28	29	30
31						

June/July

Sivan סיון

26 Sunday   20

27 Monday   21

Wrapping Cloth
Istanbul (?), Ottoman Empire, c. 1850
Silk: embroidered with metallic thread
and sequins
35½ × 35½ in. (90.2 × 90.2 cm)
The Jewish Museum, New York
Gift of Bessie Franco, 1986-122
Photo by Joseph Sachs

28 Tuesday   22

29 Wednesday   23

30 Thursday   24

1 Friday   25

Canada Day

2 Saturday   Parashat Shelah   Shabbat Mevarekhim   **26**

July

Sivan/Tammuz סיון/תמוז

3   Sunday   27

4   Monday   28

Independence Day (US)

5   Tuesday   29

6   Wednesday   Rosh Hodesh **30**

7   Thursday   Rosh Hodesh **1**

8   Friday   **2**

9   Saturday   Parashat Korah **3**

JUNE						
S	M	T	W	T	F	S
			1	2	3	4
5	6	7	8	9	10	11
12	13	14	15	16	17	18
19	20	21	22	23	24	25
26	27	28	29	30		

JULY						
S	M	T	W	T	F	S
					1	2
3	4	5	6	7	8	9
10	11	12	13	14	15	16
17	18	19	20	21	22	23
24	25	26	27	28	29	30
31						

July

Tammuz תמוז

10 Sunday   4

11 Monday   5

Tile
Keramika Workshop, Bezalel School
Jerusalem (Israel), c. 1924–30
Ceramic: painted and glazed
6¹/₁₆ × 6¹/₁₆ in. (15.4 × 15.4 cm)
The Jewish Museum, New York
Gift of Dr. Harry G. Friedman, F 1276
Photo by Richard Goodbody, Inc.

12 Tuesday   6

13 Wednesday   7

14 Thursday   8

JULY						
S	M	T	W	T	F	S
					1	2
3	4	5	6	7	8	9
10	11	12	13	14	15	16
17	18	19	20	21	22	23
24	25	26	27	28	29	30
31						

15 Friday   9

AUGUST						
S	M	T	W	T	F	S
	1	2	3	4	5	6
7	8	9	10	11	12	13
14	15	16	17	18	19	20
21	22	23	24	25	26	27
28	29	30	31			

16 Saturday   Parashat Hukkat   10

בצלאל   קרמיקה

July

Tammuz תמוז

17 Sunday   11

18 Monday   12

Bowl
Bezalel Workshops
Jerusalem (Israel), 1908–29
Silver: filigree and applique; bronze: stru
1⅜ × 8⅝ in. (3.5 × 21.9 cm)
The Jewish Museum, New York
Gift of Dr. Harry G. Friedman, F 5461
Photo by Richard Goodbody, Inc.

19 Tuesday   13

Full Moon

20 Wednesday   14

21 Thursday   15

JULY						
S	M	T	W	T	F	S
					1	2
3	4	5	6	7	8	9
10	11	12	13	14	15	16
17	18	19	20	21	22	23
24	25	26	27	28	29	30
31						

22 Friday   16

AUGUST						
S	M	T	W	T	F	S
	1	2	3	4	5	6
7	8	9	10	11	12	13
14	15	16	17	18	19	20
21	22	23	24	25	26	27
28	29	30	31			

23 Saturday   Parashat Balak   17

July

Tammuz תמוז

24 Sunday	Fast of Tammuz	**18**
25 Monday		**19**
26 Tuesday		**20**
27 Wednesday		**21**
28 Thursday		**22**
29 Friday		**23**
30 Saturday	Parashat Pinehas Shabbat Mevarekhim	**24**

Marriage Cup
#33 F
Stanley Lechtzin (American, b. 1936)
Elks Park, Pennsylvania, United States, 1989
Silver: electroformed and computer-aided manufacture
11 × 4⁹/₁₆ × 4¾ in. (27.9 × 11.6 × 12.1 cm)
The Jewish Museum, New York
Purchase: Contemporary Judaica Acquisitions Fund, 2013-8
Photo by Richard Goodbody, Inc.

July/August

Tammuz/Av תמוז/אב

31 Sunday   25

1 Monday   26

2 Tuesday   27

3 Wednesday   28

4 Thursday   29

5 Friday   Rosh Hodesh   1

6 Saturday   Parashat Mattot-Masei   2

JULY

S	M	T	W	T	F	S
					1	2
3	4	5	6	7	8	9
10	11	12	13	14	15	16
17	18	19	20	21	22	23
24	25	26	27	28	29	30
31						

AUGUST

S	M	T	W	T	F	S
	1	2	3	4	5	6
7	8	9	10	11	12	13
14	15	16	17	18	19	20
21	22	23	24	25	26	27
28	29	30	31			

August

Av אב

7 Sunday   **3**

8 Monday   **4**

Skull Cap
Bîrlad, Romania, c. 1863
Cotton: stitched and embroidered
6⅜ × 4½ in. (16.2 × 11.4 cm)
The Jewish Museum, New York
Gift of Mr. Henry and Dr. Muriel Winestine
1986-71
Photo by John Parnell

9 Tuesday   **5**

10 Wednesday   **6**

11 Thursday   **7**

AUGUST						
S	M	T	W	T	F	S
	1	2	3	4	5	6
7	8	9	10	11	12	13
14	15	16	17	18	19	20
21	22	23	24	25	26	27
28	29	30	31			

12 Friday   **8**

SEPTEMBER						
S	M	T	W	T	F	S
				1	2	3
4	5	6	7	8	9	10
11	12	13	14	15	16	17
18	19	20	21	22	23	24
25	26	27	28	29	30	

13 Saturday   Parashat Devarim   **9**
Shabbat Hazon

August

14 Sunday　　　　　　　　　　　　　　　　　　　Fast of Av **10**

Torah Ark
Urbino (Italy), c. 1500, refurbished
1624
Wood: carved and painted
94⅛ × 109¹³/₁₆ × 34 in.
(239 × 279 × 86.4 cm)
The Jewish Museum, New York
The H. Ephraim and Mordecai
Benguiat Family Collection, S 1431
Photo by Richard Goodbody, Inc.

15 Monday　　　　　　　　　　　　　　　　　　　　　　**11**

16 Tuesday　　　　　　　　　　　　　　　　　　　　　　**12**

17 Wednesday　　　　　　　　　　　　　　　　　　　　**13**

18 Thursday　　　　　　　　　　　　　　　　　　　　　**14**

AUGUST

S	M	T	W	T	F	S
	1	2	3	4	5	6
7	8	9	10	11	12	13
14	15	16	17	18	19	20
21	22	23	24	25	26	27
28	29	30	31			

Full Moon

19 Friday　　　　　　　　　　　　　　　　　　　　　　**15**

SEPTEMBER

S	M	T	W	T	F	S
				1	2	3
4	5	6	7	8	9	10
11	12	13	14	15	16	17
18	19	20	21	22	23	24
25	26	27	28	29	30	

20 Saturday　　　　　　　　　　　Parashat Va'ethannan **16**
　　　　　　　　　　　　　　　　　　　Shabbat Nahamu

August

Av אב

21 Sunday		**17**
22 Monday		**18**
23 Tuesday		**19**
24 Wednesday		**20**
25 Thursday		**21**
26 Friday		**22**
27 Saturday	Parashat Ekev Shabbat Mevarekhim	**23**

Alms Container
Boaz Yemini (Israeli, b. 1956)
Jerusalem, Israel, 1990
Silver; gold plate
8 × 3½ × 3¼ in. (20.3 × 8.9 × 8.3 cm)
The Jewish Museum, New York
Gift of the Tobe Pascher Workshop
Commission Program, 1998-118
Photo by Richard Goodbody, Inc.

August/September

28 Sunday   24

29 Monday   25

Summer Bank Holiday (UK)

30 Tuesday   26

31 Wednesday   27

1 Thursday   28

2 Friday   29

3 Saturday   Parashat Re'eh **30**
                                    Rosh Hodesh

AUGUST

S	M	T	W	T	F	S
	1	2	3	4	5	6
7	8	9	10	11	12	13
14	15	16	17	18	19	20
21	22	23	24	25	26	27
28	29	30	31			

SEPTEMBER

S	M	T	W	T	F	S
				1	2	3
4	5	6	7	8	9	10
11	12	13	14	15	16	17
18	19	20	21	22	23	24
25	26	27	28	29	30	

September

4   Sunday   Rosh Hodesh   **1**

5   Monday   **2**

Labor Day (US & Canada)

Torah Ark Curtain
Persia (?), 19th–20th century
Quilted cotton: embroidered with
silk thread
45¼ × 30⅜ in. (114.9 × 77.2 cm)
The Jewish Museum, New York
Gift of Dr. Harry G. Friedman, F 4936
Photo by Eric Pollitzer

6   Tuesday   **3**

7   Wednesday   **4**

8   Thursday   **5**

9   Friday   **6**

10   Saturday   Parashat Shofetim   **7**

SEPTEMBER

S	M	T	W	T	F	S
				1	2	3
4	5	6	7	8	9	10
11	12	13	14	15	16	17
18	19	20	21	22	23	24
25	26	27	28	29	30	

OCTOBER

S	M	T	W	T	F	S
						1
2	3	4	5	6	7	8
9	10	11	12	13	14	15
16	17	18	19	20	21	22
23	24	25	26	27	28	29
30	31					

September

Elul אלול

11 Sunday   8

12 Monday   9

Amulet Case or Sabbath Key Holder
Keter Workshop and Bezalel School
Jerusalem (Israel), 1910–20
Silver: filigree
2⅝ × 2¼ × 1 in. (6.7 × 5.7 × 2.5 cm)
The Jewish Museum, New York
Bequest of Goldie Futterman, 1999-62
Photo by Richard Goodbody, Inc.

13 Tuesday   10

14 Wednesday   11

15 Thursday   12

SEPTEMBER						
S	M	T	W	T	F	S
					1	2	3
4	5	6	7	8	9	10
11	12	13	14	15	16	17
18	19	20	21	22	23	24
25	26	27	28	29	30	

16 Friday   13

OCTOBER						
S	M	T	W	T	F	S
						1
2	3	4	5	6	7	8
9	10	11	12	13	14	15
16	17	18	19	20	21	22
23	24	25	26	27	28	29
30	31					

Full Moon

17 Saturday   Parashat Ki Teze   14

September

18 Sunday   15

19 Monday   16

Cushion Cover
The University in Jerusalem
British Mandate Palestine (Israel), c. 1925
Cotton velvet: embroidered in cotton and
wool thread
14⅞ × 17⅛ in. (37.8 × 43.5 cm)
The Jewish Museum, New York
JM 59-73b
Photo by Richard Goodbody, Inc.

20 Tuesday   17

21 Wednesday   18

International Day of Peace

22 Thursday   19

First Day of Autumn

23 Friday   20

24 Saturday   Parashat Ki Tavo / Selihot   21

September/October

Elul אלול

25 Sunday — 22

26 Monday — 23

27 Tuesday — 24

emailed Josh re yellow pages
" response to Mary re non profits.

28 Wednesday — 25

29 Thursday — 26

30 Friday — 27

1 Saturday — Parashat Nitzavim — 28

SEPTEMBER

S	M	T	W	T	F	S
				1	2	3
4	5	6	7	8	9	10
11	12	13	14	15	16	17
18	19	20	21	22	23	24
25	26	27	28	29	30	

OCTOBER

S	M	T	W	T	F	S
						1
2	3	4	5	6	7	8
9	10	11	12	13	14	15
16	17	18	19	20	21	22
23	24	25	26	27	28	29
30	31					

October

Elul/Tishri אלול/תשרי

2 Sunday   Erev Rosh ha–Shanah **29**

Rosh Hashanah
(Begins at Sundown)

3 Monday   Rosh ha–Shanah **1**

New Year Greeting
Wiener Werkstätte (Vienna, 1903–1932)
Designer: Lotte Frömel-Fochler
Printer: Brüder Kohn
Vienna (Austria), c. 1910–11
Lithograph on paper
3½ × 5½ in. (8.9 × 14 cm)
The Jewish Museum, New York
Purchase: Traditional Judaica Acquisitions
Committee Fund, 2006-6
Photo by Richard Goodbody, Inc.

4 Tuesday   Rosh ha–Shanah **2**

New Year Greeting
Wiener Werkstätte (Vienna, 1903–1932)
Designer: Wilhelm Jonasch
Printer: Brüder Kohn
Vienna (Austria), c. 1910–11
Lithograph on paper
3½ × 5½ in. (8.9 × 14 cm)
The Jewish Museum, New York
Purchase: Traditional Judaica Acquisition
Committee Fund, 2006-8
Photo by Richard Goodbody, Inc.

5 Wednesday   Fast of Gedaliah **3**

6 Thursday **4**

7 Friday **5**

8 Saturday   Parashat Vayelekh **6**
      Shabbat Shuvah

OCTOBER

S	M	T	W	T	F	S
						1
2	3	4	5	6	7	8
9	10	11	12	13	14	15
16	17	18	19	20	21	22
23	24	25	26	27	28	29
30	31					

NOVEMBER

S	M	T	W	T	F	S
		1	2	3	4	5
6	7	8	9	10	11	12
13	14	15	16	17	18	19
20	21	22	23	24	25	26
27	28	29	30			

לשנה טובה תכתבו
Herzlichen Glückwunsch
zum neuen Jahre!

לשנה טובה תכתבו
Herzlichen Glückwunsch
zum neuen Jahre!

October

Tishri תשרי

9   Sunday   7

10   Monday   8

Columbus Day (US)
Thanksgiving Day (Canada)

11   Tuesday   Erev Yom Kippur   9

Yom Kippur (Begins at Sundown)

12   Wednesday   Yom Kippur   10
                         Yizkor

13   Thursday   11

14   Friday   12

15   Saturday   Parashat Ha'azinu   13

OCTOBER

S	M	T	W	T	F	S
						1
2	3	4	5	6	7	8
9	10	11	12	13	14	15
16	17	18	19	20	21	22
23	24	25	26	27	28	29
30	31					

NOVEMBER

S	M	T	W	T	F	S
		1	2	3	4	5
6	7	8	9	10	11	12
13	14	15	16	17	18	19
20	21	22	23	24	25	26
27	28	29	30			

October

Tishri תשרי

16 Sunday   Erev Sukkot **14**

Full Moon

17 Monday   First Day of Sukkot **15**

Etrog Container
Munya Avigail Upin (American, b. 1953)
United States, 1990
Silver
5 × 8 × 6⅛ in. (12.7 × 20.3 × 15.6 cm)
The Jewish Museum, New York
Gift of the Tobe Pascher Workshop
Commission, 1998-117
Photo by Richard Goodbody, Inc.

18 Tuesday   Second Day of Sukkot **16**

19 Wednesday   Hol ha-Mo'ed Sukkot **17**

20 Thursday   Hol ha-Mo'ed Sukkot **18**

21 Friday   Hol ha-Mo'ed Sukkot **19**

22 Saturday   Hol ha-Mo'ed Sukkot **20**

October

Tishri תשרי

23 Sunday — Hoshana Rabba **21**

24 Monday — Shemini Atzeret / Yizkor **22**

25 Tuesday — Simhat Torah **23**

26 Wednesday **24**

27 Thursday **25**

28 Friday — *email to Jackie* **26**

29 Saturday — Parashat Bereshit / Shabbat Mevarekhim **27**

OCTOBER

S M T W T F S
            1
2 3 4 5 6 7 8
9 10 11 12 13 14 15
16 17 18 19 20 21 22
23 24 25 26 27 28 29
30 31

NOVEMBER

S M T W T F S
    1 2 3 4 5
6 7 8 9 10 11 12
13 14 15 16 17 18 19
20 21 22 23 24 25 26
27 28 29 30

October/November

Tishri/Heshvan תשרי/חשון

30 Sunday   **28**

---

31 Monday   **29**

Halloween

1 Tuesday   Rosh Hodesh **30**

---

2 Wednesday   Rosh Hodesh **1**

---

3 Thursday   **2**

---

4 Friday   **3**

---

5 Saturday   Parashat No'ah **4**

Kiddush Cup
Richard Fishman (American, b. 1941)
Rhode Island, United States, 1976
Silver: cast and parcel-gilt
9 × 3¾ in. (22.9 × 9.5 cm)
The Jewish Museum, New York
Gift of Abraham and Natalie Percelay
in memory of their daughter Maureen
Percelay Zusy, JM 67-76

OCTOBER

S	M	T	W	T	F	S
						1
2	3	4	5	6	7	8
9	10	11	12	13	14	15
16	17	18	19	20	21	22
23	24	25	26	27	28	29
30	31					

NOVEMBER

S	M	T	W	T	F	S
		1	2	3	4	5
6	7	8	9	10	11	12
13	14	15	16	17	18	19
20	21	22	23	24	25	26
27	28	29	30			

November

Heshvan חשון

6   Sunday   **5**

Daylight Saving Time Ends
(US & Canada)

7   Monday   **6**

Sabbath Candlesticks
Poland, 19th century
Copper alloy: cast
Each: 9 × 6¼ × 3¾ in.
(22.9 × 15.9 × 9.5 cm)
The Jewish Museum, New York
Gift of Arthur M. and Alice Chase in memory of Ida Chase (née Torchin) and her family, 2005-23a-b
Photo by Richard Goodbody, Inc.

8   Tuesday   **7**

Election Day (US)

9   Wednesday   **8**

10   Thursday   **9**

NOVEMBER						
S	M	T	W	T	F	S
		1	2	3	4	5
6	7	8	9	10	11	12
13	14	15	16	17	18	19
20	21	22	23	24	25	26
27	28	29	30			

11   Friday   **10**

DECEMBER						
S	M	T	W	T	F	S
					1	2	3
4	5	6	7	8	9	10
11	12	13	14	15	16	17
18	19	20	21	22	23	24
25	26	27	28	29	30	31

Veterans Day (US)

Remembrance Day (Canada)

12   Saturday   Parashat Lekh Lekha   **11**

November

Heshvan חשון

13 Sunday   **12**

Remembrance Sunday (UK)

14 Monday   **13**

Full Moon

15 Tuesday   **14**

Torah Scroll Cushion
Austro-Hungarian Empire, 19th century
Silk: metallic thread appliqué
11 × 14 in. (27.9 × 35.6 cm)
The Jewish Museum, New York
Gift of the Collection of Oscar and
Regina Gruss, 1994-707
Photo by John Parnell

16 Wednesday   **15**

17 Thursday   **16**

18 Friday   **17**

19 Saturday   Parashat Vayera   **18**

November

Heshvan חשון

20 Sunday   19

21 Monday   20

22 Tuesday   21

23 Wednesday   22

24 Thursday   23

NOVEMBER

S	M	T	W	T	F	S
		1	2	3	4	5
6	7	8	9	10	11	12
13	14	15	16	17	18	19
20	21	22	23	24	25	26
27	28	29	30			

Thanksgiving Day (US)

25 Friday   24

DECEMBER

S	M	T	W	T	F	S
				1	2	3
4	5	6	7	8	9	10
11	12	13	14	15	16	17
18	19	20	21	22	23	24
25	26	27	28	29	30	31

26 Saturday   Parashat Hayyei Sarah / Shabbat Mevarekhim   25

November/December   Heshvan/Kislev חשון/כסלו

27 Sunday   26

28 Monday   27

29 Tuesday   28

30 Wednesday   29

1 Thursday   Rosh Hodesh   1

NOVEMBER

S	M	T	W	T	F	S
		1	2	3	4	5
6	7	8	9	10	11	12
13	14	15	16	17	18	19
20	21	22	23	24	25	26
27	28	29	30			

2 Friday   2

DECEMBER

S	M	T	W	T	F	S
				1	2	3
4	5	6	7	8	9	10
11	12	13	14	15	16	17
18	19	20	21	22	23	24
25	26	27	28	29	30	31

3 Saturday   Parashat Toledot   3

December

Kislev כסלו

4 Sunday   4

---

5 Monday   5

Torah Binder
Germany, 1812
Linen: embroidered with silk thread
113 × 7 in. (287 × 17.8 cm)
The Jewish Museum, New York
The H. Ephraim and Mordecai Benguiat
Family Collection, S 130

---

6 Tuesday   6

---

7 Wednesday   7

---

8 Thursday   8

DECEMBER 2016

S	M	T	W	T	F	S
				1	2	3
4	5	6	7	8	9	10
11	12	13	14	15	16	17
18	19	20	21	22	23	24
25	26	27	28	29	30	31

---

9 Friday   9

JANUARY 2017

S	M	T	W	T	F	S
1	2	3	4	5	6	7
8	9	10	11	12	13	14
15	16	17	18	19	20	21
22	23	24	25	26	27	28
29	30	31				

---

10 Saturday   Parashat Vayeze 10

Human Rights Day

December

Kislev כסלו

11 Sunday   11

12 Monday   12

Torah Finial
Iran, 1946/47 (date of inscription)
Silver: pierced and engraved;
paper: ink and gouache
10⅛ × 4¼ × 1¾ in.
(25.7 × 10.8 × 4.4 cm)
The Jewish Museum, New York
Gift of Mena Rokhsar in memory of
Ebrahim Khalil Rokhsar, 1993-238
Photo by John Parnell

13 Tuesday   13

Full Moon

14 Wednesday   14

15 Thursday   15

| DECEMBER 2016 |
S	M	T	W	T	F	S
				1	2	3
4	5	6	7	8	9	10
11	12	13	14	15	16	17
18	19	20	21	22	23	24
25	26	27	28	29	30	31

16 Friday   16

| JANUARY 2017 |
S	M	T	W	T	F	S
1	2	3	4	5	6	7
8	9	10	11	12	13	14
15	16	17	18	19	20	21
22	23	24	25	26	27	28
29	30	31				

17 Saturday   Parashat Vayishlah 17

December

Kislev כסלו

18 Sunday   18

19 Monday   19

Hanukkah Lamp
F. Sussman (active 1876–1920)
Gorodnitsa (Ukraine), 1880–1920
Porcelain: glazed, painted, and gilt
$4^{13}/_{16} \times 8^{1}/_{16} \times 4^{1}/_{16}$ in.
(12.2 × 20.5 × 10.3 cm)
The Jewish Museum, New York
The Rose and Benjamin Mintz Collection
M 74
Photo by Richard Goodbody, Inc.

20 Tuesday   20

21 Wednesday   21

First Day of Winter

22 Thursday   22

23 Friday   23

24 Saturday   Parashat Vayeshev   24
Erev Hanukkah
Shabbat Mevarekhim

Hanukkah (Begins at Sundown)

DECEMBER 2016

S	M	T	W	T	F	S
				1	2	3
4	5	6	7	8	9	10
11	12	13	14	15	16	17
18	19	20	21	22	23	24
25	26	27	28	29	30	31

JANUARY 2017

S	M	T	W	T	F	S
1	2	3	4	5	6	7
8	9	10	11	12	13	14
15	16	17	18	19	20	21
22	23	24	25	26	27	28
29	30	31				

December

Kislev/Tevet כסלו/טבת

25 Sunday   First Day of Hanukkah **25**

Christmas

26 Monday   Second Day of Hanukkah **26**

Hanukkah Lamp
Miguel Oks (Argentinian, b. 1957)
New York, New York, United States, 1993
Brass: nickel-plated; stainless-steel mesh
10½ × 13¼ × 6⅛ in.
(26.7 × 33.6 × 15.5 cm)
The Jewish Museum, New York
Gift of the artist, 1994-16
Photo by John Parnell

Kwanzaa Begins
Boxing Day (Canada & UK)

27 Tuesday   Third Day of Hanukkah **27**

28 Wednesday   Fourth Day of Hanukkah **28**

29 Thursday   Fifth Day of Hanukkah **29**

30 Friday   Sixth Day of Hanukkah / Rosh Hodesh **1**

31 Saturday   Seventh Day of Hanukkah / Parashat Mi-kez **2**

DECEMBER 2016

S	M	T	W	T	F	S
				1	2	3
4	5	6	7	8	9	10
11	12	13	14	15	16	17
18	19	20	21	22	23	24
25	26	27	28	29	30	31

JANUARY 2017

S	M	T	W	T	F	S
1	2	3	4	5	6	7
8	9	10	11	12	13	14
15	16	17	18	19	20	21
22	23	24	25	26	27	28
29	30	31				

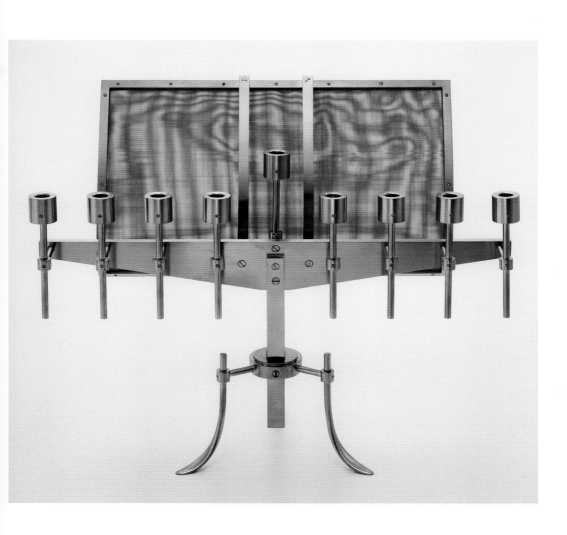

Torah and Prophetic Readings

Date	Torah Readings	Prophetic Readings
2015		
Sept. 5	Deut. 26:1–29:8	Isaiah 60:1–22
Sept. 12	Deut. 29:9–30:20	Isaiah 61:10–63:9
Sept. 14	Gen. 21:1–34; Num. 29:1–6	I Samuel 1:1–2:10
Sept. 15	Gen. 22:1–24; Num. 29:1–6	Jeremiah 31:1–19
Sept. 16	Ex. 32:11–14; 34: 1–10	(Afternoon) Isaiah 55:6–56:8
Sept. 19	Deut. 31:1–30	Hosea 14:2–10; Micah 7:18–20; Joel 2:15–27
Sept. 23	(morning) Lev. 16:1-34; Num. 29:7–11	Isaiah 57:14–58:14
	(afternoon) Lev. 18:1-34	Jonah 1:1–4:11; Micah 7:18–20
Sept. 26	Deut. 32:1–52	II Samuel 22:1–51
Sept. 28	Lev. 22:26–23:44; Num. 29:12–16	Zech. 14:1–21
Sept. 29	Lev. 22:26–23:44; Num. 29:12–16	I Kings 8:2–21
Sept. 30	Num. 29:17–25	
Oct. 1	Num. 29:20–28	
Oct. 2	Num. 29:23–31	
Oct. 3	Ex. 33:12-34:26; Num. 29: 26-31	Ezek. 38:18-39:16
Oct. 4	Num. 29:26–34	
Oct. 5	Deut. 14:22–16:17; Num. 29:35–30:1	I Kings 8:45–9:1
Oct. 6	Deut. 33:1–34:12; Gen. 1:1–2:3; Num. 29:35–30:1	Joshua 1:1–18
Oct. 10	Gen. 1:1–6:8	Isaiah 42:5–43:10
Oct. 13	Num. 28:1–15	
Oct. 14	Num. 28:1–15	
Oct. 17	Gen. 6:9–11:32	Isaiah 54:1–55:5
Oct. 24	Gen. 12:1–17:27	Isaiah 40:27–41:16
Oct. 31	Gen 18:1–22:24	II Kings 4:1–37
Nov. 7	Gen. 23:1–25:18	I Kings 1:1–31
Nov. 12	Num. 28:1–15	
Nov. 13	Num. 28:1–15	
Nov. 14	Gen. 25:19–28:9	Malachi 1:1–2:7
Nov. 21	Gen. 28:10–32:3	Hosea 12:13–14:10
Nov. 28	Gen. 32:4–36:43	Obadiah 1:1–21
Dec. 5	Gen. 37:1–40:23	Amos 2:6–3:8
Dec. 7	Num. 7:1–17	
Dec. 8	Num. 7:18–29	
Dec. 9	Num. 7:24–35	
Dec. 10	Num. 7:30–41	
Dec. 11	Num. 7:36–47	
Dec. 12	Gen 41:1–44; Num. 28:9–15; Num. 7:42–47	Zech. 2:14–4:7
Dec. 13	Num. 28: 1–15; Num. 7:48–53	
Dec. 14	Num. 7:54–8:4	
Dec. 19	Gen. 44:18–47:27	Ezek. 37:15–28
Dec. 22	(morning) Ex. 32:11–14; 34:1–10	
	(afternoon) Ex. 31:11–14; 34: 1–10	Isaiah 55:6–56:8
Dec. 26	Gen 47:28–50:26	I Kings 2:1–2:12
2016		
Jan. 2	Ex. 1:1–6:1	Isaiah 27:6–28:13; 29:22–23
Jan. 9	Ex. 6:2–9:35	Ezek. 28:25–29:21
Jan. 11	Num. 28:1–15	
Jan. 16	Ex. 10:1–13:16	Jeremiah 46:13–28
Jan. 23	Ex. 13:17–17:16	Judges 4:4–5:31
Jan. 30	Ex. 18:1–20:23	Isaiah 6:1–7:6; 9:5–6
Feb. 6	Ex. 21:1–24:18	Jeremiah 34:8–22; 33:25–26
Feb. 9	Num. 28:1–15	
Feb. 10	Num. 28:1–15	
Feb. 13	Ex. 25:1–27:19	I Kings 5:26–6:13
Feb. 20	Ex. 27:20–30:10	Ezek. 43:10–27
Feb. 27	Ex. 30:11–34:35	I Kings 18:1–39
Mar. 5	Ex. 35:1–38:20; 30:11–16	II Kings 12:1–17
Mar. 10	Num. 28:1–15	
Mar. 11	Num. 28:1–15	
Mar. 12	Ex. 38:21–40:38	I Kings 7:51–8:21
Mar. 19	Lev. 1:1–5:26; Deut. 25:17–19	I Sam. 15:2–34
Mar. 23	Ex. 32:11–14; 34:1–10	(afternoon) Isaiah 55:6–56:8
Mar. 24	Ex. 17:8–16	
Mar. 26	Lev. 6:1–8:36	Jeremiah 7:21–8:3; 9:22–23
Apr. 2	Lev. 9:1–11:47; Num.19: 1-22	Ezek. 36:16-38
Apr. 9	Lev. 12:1–13:59; Num. 28:9–15; Ex. 12:1–20	Ezek. 45:16–46:18
Apr. 16	Lev. 14:1–15:33	Malachi 3:4–24
Apr. 23	Ex. 12:21–51; Num. 28:16–25	Joshua 5:2–6:1
Apr. 24	Lev. 22:26–23:44; Num. 28:16–25	II Kings 23:1–9; 23:21–25

Date	Torah Readings	Prophetic Readings
2016		
Apr. 25	Ex. 13:1–16; Num. 28:19–25	
Apr. 26	Ex. 22:24–23:19; Num. 28:19–25	
Apr. 27	Ex. 34:1–26; Num. 28:19–25	
Apr. 28	Num. 9:1–14; 28:19–25	
Apr. 29	Ex. 13:17–15:26; Num. 28:19–25	II Sam. 22:1–51
Apr. 30	Deut. 14:22–16:17; Num. 28:19–25	Isaiah 10:32–12:6
May 7	Lev. 16:1–18:30	I Sam. 20:18–42
May 8	Num. 28:1–15	
May 9	Num. 28:1–15	
May 14	Lev. 19:1–20:27	Amos 9:7–15
May 21	Lev. 21:1–24:23	Ezek. 44:15–31
May 28	Lev. 25:1–26:2	Jeremiah 32:6–27
June 4	Lev. 26:3–27:34	Jeremiah 16:19–17:14
June 7	Num. 28:1–15	
June 11	Num. 1:1–4:20	Hosea 2:1–22
June 12	Ex. 19:1–20:23; Num. 28:26–31	Ezek. 1:1–28; 3:12
June 13	Deut. 15:19–16:17; Num. 28:26–31	Habakkuk 2:20–3:19
June 18	Num. 4:21–7:89	Judges 13:2–25
June 25	Num. 8:1–12:16	Zech. 2:14–4:7
July 2	Num. 13:1–15:41	Joshua 2:1–24
July 6	Num. 28:1–15	
July 7	Num. 28:1–15	
July 9	Num. 16:1–18:32	I Samuel 11:14–12:22
July 16	Num. 19:1–22:1	Judges 11:1–33
July 23	Num. 22:2–25:9	Micah 5:6–6:8
July 24	Ex. 32:11–14; 34:1–10	(afternoon) Isaiah 55:5–56:8
July 30	Num. 25:10–30:1	Jeremiah 1:1–2:3
Aug. 5	Num. 28:1–15	
Aug. 6	Num. 30:2–36:13	Jeremiah 2:4–28; 3:4
Aug. 13	Deut. 1:1–3:22	Isaiah 1:1–27
Aug. 14	(morning) Deut. 4:25–40	Jeremiah 8:13–9:23
Aug. 14	(afternoon) Ex. 32:11–14; 34:1–10	Isaiah 55:6–56:8
Aug. 20	Deut. 3:23–7:11	Isaiah 40:1–26
Aug. 27	Deut. 7:12–11:25	Isaiah 49:14–51:3
Sept. 3	Deut. 11:26–16:17; Num. 28: 1–10	Isaiah 66:1–24
Sept. 4	Num. 28:1–15	
Sept. 10	Deut. 16:18–21:9	Isaiah 51:12–52:12
Sept. 17	Deut. 21:10–25:19	Isaiah 54:1–10
Sept. 24	Deut. 26:1–29:8	Isaiah 60:1–22
Oct. 1	Deut. 29:9–30:20	Isaiah 61:10–63:9
Oct. 3	Gen. 21:1–34; Num. 29:1–6	I Samuel 1:1–2:10
Oct. 4	Gen. 22:1–24; Num. 29:1–6	Jeremiah 31:1–19
Oct. 5	Ex. 32:11–14; 34:1–10	(afternoon) Isaiah 55:6–56:8
Oct. 8	Deut. 31:1–30	Hosea 14:2–10; Micah 7:18–20; Joel 2:15–27
Oct. 12	(morning) Lev. 16:1–34; Num. 29:7–11	Isaiah 57:14–58:14
Oct. 12	(afternoon) Lev. 18:1–30	Jonah 1:1–4:11; Micah 7:18–20
Oct. 15	Deut. 32:1–52	II Samuel 22:1–51
Oct. 17	Lev. 22:26–23:44; Num. 29:12–16	Zech. 14:1–21
Oct. 18	Lev. 22:26–23:44; Num. 29:12–16	I Kings 8:2–21
Oct. 19	Num. 29:17–22	
Oct. 20	Num. 29:20–28	
Oct. 21	Num. 29: 23–31	
Oct. 22	Ex. 33:12–34:26; Num. 29:29–31	Ezek. 38:18–39:16
Oct. 23	Num. 29:26–34	
Oct. 24	Deut. 14:22–16:17; Num. 29:35–30:1	I Kings 8:54–9:1
Oct. 25	Deut. 33:1–34:12; Gen. 1:1–2:3; Num. 29:35–30:1	Joshua 1:1–18
Oct. 29	Gen. 1:1–6:8	Isaiah 42:5–43:10
Nov. 1	Num. 28:1–15	
Nov. 2	Num. 28:1–15	
Nov. 5	Gen. 6:9–11:32	Isaiah 54:1–55:5
Nov. 12	Gen. 12:1–17:27	Isaiah 40:27–41:16
Nov. 19	Gen. 18:1–22:24	II Kings 4:1–37
Nov. 26	Gen. 23:1–25:18	I Kings 1:1–31
Dec. 1	Num. 28:1–15	
Dec. 3	Gen. 25:19–28:9	Malachi 1:1–2:7
Dec. 10	Gen. 28:10–32:3	Hosea 12:13–14:10
Dec. 17	Gen. 32:4–36:43	Obadiah 1:1–21
Dec. 24	Gen. 37:1–40:23	Amos 2:6–3:8
Dec. 25	Num. 7:1–17	
Dec. 26	Num. 7:18–29	
Dec. 27	Num. 7:24–35	
Dec. 28	Num. 7:30–41	
Dec. 29	Num. 7:36–47	
Dec. 30	Num. 28:1–15; 7:42–47	
Dec. 31	Gen. 41:1–44:17; Num.7:48–53	Zech. 2:14–4:6

Jewish Holidays

	Hebrew Date	Candle Blessings	Torah Readings	Prophetic Readings	Additional Readings
Rosh ha-Shanah (The New Year)	Tishri 1 & 2 First day can fall only on Monday, Tuesday, Thursday, Saturday	1,2	First day: Gen. 21:1–34; Num. 29:1-6 Second day: Gen. 22:1–24; Num. 29:1–6	First day: I Samuel 1:1–2:10 Second day: Jeremiah 31:1–19	Mahzor (special prayer book) for Rosh Hashanah
Tzom Gedaliah (Fast of Gedaliah)	Tishri 3		Ex. 32:11–14; 34:1–10	Afternoon: Isaiah 55:6–56:8	‡ "Answer us, O Lord, answer us."
Yom Kippur (Day of Atonement)	Tishri 10 Can fall only on Monday, Wednesday, Thursday, Saturday	1a,2	Morning: Lev. 16:1–34; Num. 29:7–11 Afternoon: Lev. 18:1–30	Morning: Isaiah 57:14–58:14 Afternoon: Jonah 1–4; Micah 7:18–20	Mahzor for Yom Kippur; Yizkor (memorial prayers)
Sukkot (Tabernacles)	Tishri 15–21 Can fall only on Monday, Tuesday, Thursday, Saturday	1,2	Lev. 22:26–23:44; Num. 29:12–16	First day: Zechariah 14:1–21 Second day: I Kings 8:2–21	Full Hallel on all days §"... May there come before you ..." Book of Ecclesiastes Lulav and etrog Kohelet ★★★
Shemini Atzeret (The Eighth Day's Assembly)	Tishri 22 Can fall only on Monday, Tuesday, Thursday, Saturday	1,2	Deut. 14:22–16:17; Num. 29:35–30:1	I Kings 8:54–9:1	Hallel Prayer for rain "... May there come before you ..." Yizkor
Simhat Torah (Rejoicing of the Torah)	Tishri 23 Can fall only on Sunday, Tuesday, Wednesday, Friday	1,2	Deut. 33:1–34:12; Gen. 1:1–2:3; Num. 29:35–30:1	Joshua 1:1–18	Hallel § "... May there come before you ..."
Hanukkah	Kislev 25– Tevet 3	3,4,2#	See note†	First Shabbat: Zechariah 2:14–4:7 Second Shabbat (when there is one): I Kings 7:40–50	Full Hallel on all days || "... On the miracles ..."
Fast of the Tenth of the Month of Tevet	Tevet 10		Ex. 32:11–14; 34:1–10	Afternoon: Isaiah 55:6–56:8	‡ "Answer us, O Lord, answer us ..."
Tu B'Shevat (New Year for the Trees)	Shevat 15				
Ta'anit Esther (Fast of Esther)	Adar 13		Ex. 32:11–14; 34:1–10	Afternoon: Isaiah 55:6–56:8	‡ "Answer us, O Lord, answer us ..."

Theme or Element	Biblical/Historial Significance	Seasonal Significance	Mood/Setting	Selected Customs
Creation World is judged regarding people "On Rosh Hashanah it is written . . ." "Today is the birthday of the world"	"And in the seventh month, on the first day of the month, you shall have a holy convocation . . ." —Num. 29:1–6	Beginning of end of productive year	Putting behind to start anew Community Steady high	Dipping apples in honey Sending wishes for a good and a sweet year Casting crumbs (sin) into the river Blowing shofar Round hallah
Divine displeasure	Assassination of Gedaliah, governor of Judah, who had been appointed by Nebuchadnezzar, 586 B.C.		Human supplication for mercy Mild low	Fasting from morning to evening
Humanity is judged Prayer/charity/repentance "And on Yom Kippur it is sealed . . ."	"And on the tenth day of this seventh month you shall have a holy convocation; and you shall afflict your souls: You shall do no manner of work . . ." —Num. 29:7–11		Introspection Returning self before God Heavy high	Charity Fasting and abstinence Wearing white garments
Redemption Sukkat Shalom (Tabernacle of Peace) Hospitality Foretaste of messianic harmony	Israelites wandering through the desert "And on the fifteenth day of the seventh month you shall have a holy convocation . . ." —Num. 29:12–34	Final harvest festival Preparation for winter hibernation	Brotherhood/sister-hood/peoplehood Joy	Eating (sleeping) in the sukkah Inviting guests Waving the lulav and etrog
World is judged regarding the availability of water	"On the eighth day you shall have a solemn assembly . . ." —Num. 29:35–39	Apprehension con-cerning there being a good rainy season to prepare the land for the next growing period	Collective concern Low	
Torah is cosmic teaching Circularity (never-ending circle of Torah and of the Jewish year)			Wedding ceremony "Happy are we! How goodly is our portion, how pleasant our lot, how beautiful our heritage . . ." Ecstasy	Dancing with the Torah Children carrying flags and apples Getting high (drunk) on Torah
Spreading light	Defeat of Syrians by Maccabees; cleansing of the Temple; rededicating the people to Judaism, 167 B.C.	Winter solstice Midwinter fire festival	Emergence from darkness to light Light high	Lighting candles Playing dreidel Eating potato latkes
Divine displeasure	Commencement of siege of Jerusalem by Nebuchadnezzar, 586 B.C.		Human supplication for mercy Mild low	Fasting from morning to evening
Reawakening of nature Reestablishing the divine flow	Date from which to count the years of the tree for purposes of tithe Dedication of first fruits Personal use of the fruits	First signs of spring Sap begins rising in trees in Israel	Good fruits Rich soil Sensuous high	Planting trees Eating varieties of nuts and fruits, especially carob
Supplication	Jews of Persia praying for overturning of Haman's plot to destroy them			Fasting from morning to evening

	Hebrew Date	Candle Blessings	Torah Readings	Prophetic Readings	Additional Readings
Purim (Feast of Lots)	Adar 14		Ex. 17:8–16		Book of Esther || "... On the miracles ..."
Pesah (Passover)	Nisan 15–22 First day can fall only on Sunday, Tuesday, Thursday, Saturday	1,2★★	First day: Ex. 12:21–51; Num. 28:16–25 Second day: Lev. 22:26–23:44; Num. 28:16–25 Seventh day: Ex. 13:17–15:26; Num. 28:19–25 Eighth day: Deut. 15:19–16:17; Num. 28:19–25*	First day: Joshua 3:5–7; 5:2–6:1 Second day: II Kings 23:1–9, 21–25 Seventh day: II Samuel 22:1–51 Eighth day: Isaiah 10:32–12:6	Full Hallel first two days Partial Hallel last six days § "... May there come before you ..." Song of Songs Yizkor last day
Omer	Nisan 16– Sivan 5				
Yom ha-Shoah (Day of Remembrance of the Holocaust)	Nisan 27				
Yom ha-Atzma'ut (Israel Independence Day)	Iyar 5				Hallel
Lag B'omer (33rd Day in Omer Count)	Iyar 18				
Shavuot (Feast of Weeks)	Sivan 6–7 First day can fall only on Sunday, Monday, Wednesday, Friday	1,2	First day: Ex. 19:1–20:23; Num. 28:26–31 Second day: Deut. 15:19–16:17★; Num. 28: 26–31	First day: Ezekiel 1:1–28, 3:12 Second day: Habakkuk 2:20–3:19	Full Hallel § "... May there come before you .. Book of Ruth Yizkor second day
Fast of the Seventeenth of the Month of Tammuz	Tammuz 17		Ex. 32:11–14, 34:1–10	Afternoon: Isaiah 55:6–56:8	‡ "Answer us, O Lord, answer us ..."
Tisha B'Av	Av 9		Deut. 4:25–40 Afternoon: Ex. 32:11–14, 34:1–10	Morning: Jeremiah 8:13–9:23 Isaiah 55:6–56:8	Book of Lamentations
Rosh Hodesh (The New Moon)			Num. 28:1–15		Partial Hallel § "... May there come before you ..

★ If the last day of Pesah or the second day of Shavuot falls on Shabbat, there is a special Torah reading: Deut. 14:22–16:17.

† On Hanukkah, essentially what is read is Num. 7:1–8:4, a description of the offerings made by the princes of the twelve tribes at the time the Tabernacle was dedicated in the desert. This serves as the paradigm for the rededication celebration of Hanukkah. The basic order is Day 1, Num 7:1–17; Day 2, Num 7:18–29; Day 3, Num. 7:24–35; Day 4, Num. 7:30–41; Day 5, Num. 7:36–47; Day 6, Num. 7:42–53; Day 7, Num. 7:48–59; Day 8, Num. 7:54–84. Because the New Moon (either one or two days) occurs during the holiday, as does either one Shabbat or two Shabbatot, and because the New Moon and Shabbat can coincide, it is too difficult to list all the Torah readings for all eventualities. Consequently, one must check each year for the correct Torah readings for Hanukkah for that year.

‡ "Answer us, O Lord, answer us ..." (Anenu) is a special prayer added to the Amidah (standing devotion) on fast days entreating God to deliver us from our troubles.

§ "... May there come before you ..." (Ya'aleh v'Yavo)—a prayer added to the Amidah and Birkat Hamazon (grace after meals) on festivals and New Moons—petitions God to remember the whole House of Israel for good and blessing so that our festivals may be celebrated in joy.

Theme or Element	Biblical/Historial Significance	Seasonal Significance	Mood/Setting	Selected Customs
Giving gifts Giving charity Overcoming duality	Victory of Jews over Haman through the intercession of Esther and Mordecai	Spring rites festival	Breaking of inhibitions, getting so drunk as not to distinguish between "Blessed Mordecai and cursed Haman" Dionysian high	Blotting out Haman's name with graggers Sending gifts of food to friends Giving to the poor
Creation/Revelation World is judged regarding produce Freedom Birth—breaking out	Redemption of Israelites from Egyptian slavery "And in the first month, on the fourteenth day of the month, is the Lord's Passover . . ." —Num. 28:16–25	New Year festival: first month of year First crops (barley) First calvings	Family Reflective Liberation through discipline Serious high	Removing hametz (leaven) Eating matzah Participating in a seder
Growth Counting Anticipating	"And you shall count unto you from the morrow after the day of rest . . . seven weeks . . ." Plague on disciples of R. Akiba, 2nd century	Apprehension concerning fate of latter crops—will the seed take? Lev. 23:15–16	Semi-mourning Expectant, sober Anticipation	Counting the days
God is judged	The destruction of six million Jews during World War II while the world, God, and man remained silent		Reflective Somber	
Strength	Declaration of an independent state of Israel in 1948		Secular joy	Parades
Release from mourning Spring festival	The plague of R. Akiba's disciples lifted	Spring outing	Springtime Fantasy, fancy, and frolic	Picnics
Revelation World is judged regarding fruits Maturity Receiving	Giving of the Torah to Israelites at Mt. Sinai "When you bring a new meal offering unto the Lord in your feast of weeks, you shall have a holy convocation . . ." —Num. 28:28–31	First reapings of fruits and produce	Community Openness, sharing, receptivity Climactic high	Staying up all night studying Torah Spreading grasses in synagogue Dairy products
Divine displeasure	Moses breaks the first tablets First breach in Jerusalem's walls by Nebuchadnezzar's forces		Human supplication for mercy Mild low	Fasting from morning to evening
Contemplating the ashes upon which the new world will rise Mourning	Destruction of the First and Second Temples—586 B.C. and 70 A.D.		Somber mourning Heavy	Fasting Sitting on the floor Singing dirges
Renewal		Reemergence of the moon after its three-day withdrawal	Semi-holiday for women Light	

|| ". . . on the miracles . . ." (Al Hanisim) is a prayer added to the Amidah and Birkat Hamazon during Hanukkah and Purim, thanking God for the miracles he performed for our ancestors and for us.
Candle blessings:
1. Blessed are You, Adonai our God, Ruler of the Universe, who has sanctified us with His commandments and commanded us to light the [Shabbat and] Festival light.
1a. Blessed are You, Adonai our God, Ruler of the Universe, who has sanctified us with His commandments and commanded us to light the Yom Kippur light.
2. Blessed are You, Adonai our God, Ruler of the Universe, who has given us life and preserved us and enabled us to reach this season.
3. Blessed are You, Adonai our God, Ruler of the Universe, who has sanctified us with His commandments and commanded us to light the Hanukkah lights.
4. Blessed are you, Adonai our God, Ruler of the Universe, who has done great miracles for our ancestors, in those days, at this time.
First night of Hanukkah only.
★★ On the last two nights of Pesah, only the first blessing is said.
★★★ When Shemini Atzeret falls on Shabbat, Kohelet is read then.

Holidays Begin at Sundown on the Preceding Day

	2016	2017	2018	2019	2020	2021	2022
Purim	March 24	March 12	March 1	March 21	March 10	Feb. 26	March 17
Pesah	April 23	April 11	March 31	April 20	April 9	March 28	April 16
Lag ba-Omer	May 26	May 14	May 3	May 23	May 12	April 30	May 19
Shavuot	June 12	May 31	May 20	June 9	May 29	May 17	June 5
Rosh ha-Shanah	Oct. 3	Sept. 21	Sept. 10	Sept. 30	Sept. 19	Sept. 7	Sept. 26
Yom Kippur	Oct. 12	Sept. 30	Sept. 19	Oct. 9	Sept. 28	Sept. 16	Oct. 5
Sukkot	Oct. 17	Oct. 5	Sept. 24	Oct. 14	Oct. 3	Sept. 21	Oct. 10
Shemini Atzeret	Oct. 24	Oct. 12	Oct. 1	Oct. 21	Oct. 10	Sept. 28	Oct. 17
Simhat Torah	Oct. 25	Oct. 13	Oct. 2	Oct. 22	Oct. 11	Sept. 29	Oct. 18
Hanukkah	Dec. 25	Dec. 13	Dec. 3	Dec. 23	Dec. 11	Nov. 29	Dec. 19

	2023	2024	2025	2026	2027	2028	2029
Purim	March 7	March 24	March 14	March 3	March 23	March 12	March 1
Pesah	April 6	April 23	April 13	April 2	April 22	April 11	March 31
Lag ba-Omer	May 9	May 26	May 16	May 5	May 25	May 14	May 3
Shavuot	May 26	June 12	June 2	May 22	June 11	May 31	May 20
Rosh ha-Shanah	Sept. 16	Oct. 3	Sept. 23	Sept. 12	Oct. 2	Sept. 21	Sept. 10
Yom Kippur	Sept. 25	Oct. 12	Oct. 2	Sept. 21	Oct. 11	Sept. 30	Sept. 19
Sukkot	Sept. 30	Oct. 17	Oct. 7	Sept. 26	Oct. 16	Oct. 5	Sept. 24
Shemini Atzeret	Oct. 7	Oct. 24	Oct. 14	Oct. 3	Oct. 23	Oct. 12	Oct. 1
Simhat Torah	Oct. 8	Oct. 25	Oct. 15	Oct. 4	Oct. 24	Oct. 13	Oct. 2
Hanukkah	Dec. 8	Dec. 26	Dec. 15	Dec. 5	Dec. 25	Dec. 13	Dec. 2

Shabbat and Holiday Candle-Lighting Times for September 2015 through December 2016

2015	Jerusalem	London GMT	N.Y.C. EST	Phila. EST	Wash., D.C. EST	Miami EST	Toronto EST	Houston CST	Detroit EST	Chicago CST	L.A. PST
Sept. 4	6:21	7:22	7:05	7:09	7:16	7:19	7:30	7:23	7:43	7:01	6:57
Sept. 11	6:11	7:07	6:54	6:58	7:05	7:11	7:17	7:14	7:31	6:49	6:47
Sept. 13	6:09	7:02	6:50	6:55	7:02	7:09	7:14	7:12	7:28	6:45	6:44
Sept. 14		8:00	7:49	7:53	8:00	8:08	8:12	8:11	8:26	7:44	7:43
Sept. 18	6:02	6:50	6:42	6:46	6:54	7:03	7:04	7:05	7:19	6:37	6:37
Sept. 22	5:57	6:41	6:35	6:40	6:47	6:59	6:57	7:00	7:12	6:30	6:32
Sept. 25	5:53	6:34	6:30	6:35	6:42	6:56	6:52	6:57	7:06	6:24	6:27
Sept. 27	5:50	6:30	6:27	6:31	6:39	6:54	6:48	6:54	7:03	6:21	6:25
Sept. 28		7:28	7:25	7:30	7:38	7:53	7:47	7:54	8:02	7:20	7:24
Oct. 2	5:44	6:18	6:18	6:23	6:31	6:48	6:39	6:48	6:54	6:12	6:18
Oct. 4	5:41	6:14	6:15	6:20	6:28	6:46	6:35	6:46	6:51	6:09	6:15
Oct. 5		7:12	7:14	7:19	7:27	7:45	7:34	7:45	7:50	7:08	7:14
Oct. 9	5:35	6:04	6:07	6:12	6:20	6:41	6:26	6:40	6:42	6:01	6:08
Oct. 16	5:27	5:47	5:56	6:02	6:10	6:34	6:14	6:32	6:31	5:49	5:59
Oct. 23	5:19	5:33	5:46	5:52	6:00	6:28	6:03	6:25	6:20	5:39	5:51
Oct. 30	4:12	4:19	5:36	5:42	5:52	6:22	5:53	6:19	6:10	5:29	5:44
Nov. 6	4:07	4:07	4:28	4:34	4:44	5:18	4:44	5:13	5:01	4:20	4:37
Nov. 13	4:02	3:56	4:21	4:28	4:38	5:14	4:36	5:09	4:54	4:13	4:32
Nov. 20	3:58	3:47	4:16	4:23	4:33	5:12	4:30	5:06	4:48	4:07	4:28
Nov. 27	3:56	3:40	4:12	4:19	4:29	5:11	4:25	5:04	4:44	4:03	4:26
Dec. 4	3:56	3:35	4:10	4:17	4:28	5:11	4:23	5:04	4:42	4:01	4:25
Dec. 11	3:57	3:33	4:10	4:17	4:28	5:12	4:22	5:05	4:41	4:01	4:26
Dec. 18	3:59	3:34	4:12	4:19	4:30	5:15	4:24	5:07	4:43	4:03	4:28
Dec. 25	4:02	3:37	4:15	4:22	4:33	5:18	4:27	5:11	4:47	4:06	4:31

2016	Jerusalem	London	N.Y.C.	Phila.	Wash., D.C.	Miami	Toronto	Houston	Detroit	Chicago	L.A.
		GMT	EST	EST	EST	EST	EST	CST	EST	CST	PST
Jan. 1	4:27	3:43	4:20	4:27	4:38	5:23	4:33	5:13	4:50	4:10	4:34
Jan. 8	4:33	3:51	4:27	4:34	4:44	5:28	4:39	5:18	4:56	4:16	4:40
Jan. 15	4:39	4:01	4:34	4:41	4:51	5:33	4:47	5:24	5:04	4:24	4:46
Jan. 22	4:45	4:13	4:42	4:49	4:59	5:38	4:56	5:30	5:12	4:32	4:53
Jan. 29	4:51	4:25	4:51	4:57	5:07	5:43	5:06	5:36	5:21	4:41	5:00
Feb. 5	4:58	4:38	5:00	5:06	5:15	5:49	5:15	5:42	5:31	4:50	5:07
Feb. 12	5:04	4:51	5:08	5:14	5:23	5:53	5:25	5:47	5:40	4:59	5:13
Feb. 19	5:10	5:03	5:17	5:22	5:31	5:58	5:34	5:53	5:49	5:08	5:20
Feb. 26	5:16	5:16	5:25	5:30	5:39	6:02	5:43	5:58	5:57	5:16	5:26
Mar. 4	5:21	5:28	5:33	5:38	5:46	6:06	5:52	6:03	6:06	5:25	5:32
Mar. 11	5:26	5:40	5:40	5:45	5:53	6:09	6:01	6:07	6:14	5:33	5:38
Mar. 18	5:31	5:52	6:48	6:53	7:00	7:13	7:10	7:11	7:22	6:41	6:43
Mar. 25	5:36	6:04	6:55	7:00	7:07	7:16	7:18	7:16	7:30	6:48	6:48
Apr. 1	6:40	7:16	7:03	7:07	7:14	7:19	7:27	7:20	7:38	6:56	6:54
Apr. 8	6:45	7:28	7:10	7:14	7:20	7:22	7:35	7:24	7:46	7:04	6:59
Apr. 15	6:50	7:39	7:17	7:21	7:27	7:26	7:43	7:28	7:54	7:12	7:04
Apr. 22	6:55	7:51	7:25	7:28	7:34	7:29	7:52	7:33	8:02	7:19	7:10
Apr. 23	8:26	8:53	8:26	8:30	8:35	8:30	8:53	9:06	9:35	8:53	8:43
Apr. 28	6:59	8:01	7:31	7:34	7:41	7:32	7:59	7:36	8:08	7:26	7:15
Apr. 29	6:59	8:03	7:32	7:35	7:35	7:33	8:00	7:37	8:10	7:27	7:15
May. 6	7:04	8:14	7:39	7:42	7:47	7:36	8:08	7:42	8:17	7:35	7:21
May. 13	7:09	8:25	7:46	7:49	7:54	7:40	8:16	7:46	8:25	7:42	7:26
May. 20	7:14	8:35	7:53	7:56	8:00	7:44	8:23	7:50	8:32	7:49	7:31
May. 27	7:19	8:44	7:59	8:01	8:06	7:47	8:30	7:55	8:38	7:55	7:36
Jun. 3	7:22	8:52	8:04	8:07	8:11	7:51	8:36	7:58	8:44	8:01	7:40
Jun. 10	7:26	8:58	8:08	8:11	8:15	7:54	8:40	8:01	8:48	8:05	7:44
Jun. 12	8:27	10:00	9:10	9:12	9:16	8:55	9:42	9:35	10:22	9:38	9:17
Jun. 17	7:28	9:02	8:11	8:13	8:18	7:56	8:43	8:04	8:51	8:08	7:46
Jun. 24	7:30	9:03	8:13	8:15	8:19	7:57	8:45	8:05	8:52	8:09	7:48
Jul. 1	7:30	9:02	8:12	8:15	8:19	7:58	8:44	8:06	8:52	8:09	7:48
Jul. 8	7:29	8:58	8:11	8:13	8:17	7:57	8:42	8:05	8:50	8:07	7:47
Jul. 15	7:27	8:52	8:07	8:10	8:14	7:56	8:38	8:03	8:46	8:03	7:44
Jul. 22	7:24	8:44	8:02	8:05	8:09	7:53	8:32	8:00	8:41	7:58	7:40
Jul. 29	7:19	8:34	7:56	7:58	8:03	7:50	8:25	7:55	8:34	7:51	7:35
Aug. 5	7:14	8:22	7:48	7:51	7:56	7:45	8:16	7:50	8:26	7:43	7:29
Aug. 12	7:07	8:10	7:39	7:42	7:48	7:40	8:07	7:44	8:16	7:34	7:22
Aug. 19	7:00	7:56	7:29	7:32	7:38	7:34	7:56	7:37	8:06	7:23	7:14
Aug. 26	6:52	7:41	7:18	7:22	7:28	7:27	7:44	7:29	7:55	7:12	7:05
Sept. 2	6:43	7:25	7:07	7:11	7:18	7:20	7:32	7:21	7:43	7:01	6:56
Sept. 9	6:34	7:09	6:56	7:00	7:07	7:12	7:19	7:13	7:31	6:49	6:47
Sept. 16	6:25	6:53	6:44	6:48	6:56	7:05	7:07	7:04	7:19	6:37	6:37
Sept. 23	5:16	6:37	6:32	6:37	6:44	6:57	6:54	6:56	7:06	6:25	6:27
Sept. 30	5:07	6:21	6:20	6:25	6:33	6:49	6:41	6:47	6:54	6:13	6:17
Oct. 2	5:04	6:17	6:17	6:22	6:30	6:47	6:37	6:45	6:51	6:09	6:15
Oct. 3	6:03	7:15	7:16	7:21	7:29	7:47	7:36	8:16	8:21	7:40	7:46
Oct. 7	4:58	6:05	6:09	6:14	6:22	6:42	6:29	6:39	6:42	6:01	6:08
Oct. 11	4:53	5:57	6:03	6:08	6:16	6:38	6:22	6:34	6:35	5:54	6:03
Oct. 14	4:49	5:50	5:58	6:03	6:12	6:35	6:17	6:31	6:30	5:49	5:59
Oct. 16	4:47	5:46	5:55	6:00	6:09	6:33	6:13	6:29	6:27	5:46	5:56
Oct. 17	5:46	6:44	6:54	6:59	7:08	7:33	7:12	8:00	7:58	7:17	7:28
Oct. 21	4:41	5:53	5:48	5:53	6:02	6:29	6:05	6:24	6:20	5:39	5:50
Oct. 23	4:39	5:31	5:45	5:51	5:59	6:27	6:02	6:22	6:17	5:36	5:48
Oct. 24	5:39	6:30	6:44	6:50	6:59	7:27	7:01	7:53	7:48	7:07	7:20
Oct. 28	4:34	5:22	5:38	5:44	5:53	6:23	5:55	6:17	6:10	5:29	5:43
Nov. 4	4:28	4:09	5:30	5:36	5:45	6:18	5:45	6:11	6:01	5:20	5:36
Nov. 11	4:23	3:58	4:23	4:29	4:39	5:15	4:37	5:07	4:53	4:13	4:31
Nov. 18	4:20	3:48	4:17	4:23	4:33	5:12	4:31	5:04	4:47	4:07	4:27
Nov. 25	4:17	3:41	4:13	4:19	4:30	5:11	4:26	5:02	4:42	4:02	4:24
Dec. 2	4:16	3:36	4:10	4:17	4:28	5:11	4:23	5:03	4:42	4:02	4:25
Dec. 9	4:17	3:33	4:10	4:17	4:28	5:12	4:22	5:04	4:41	4:01	4:25
Dec. 16	4:19	3:33	4:11	4:18	4:29	5:14	4:23	5:06	4:42	4:02	4:27
Dec. 23	4:22	3:36	4:15	4:22	4:32	5:18	4:27	5:07	4:44	4:04	4:29
Dec. 30	4:26	3:42	4:19	4:26	4:37	5:22	4:32	5:14	4:51	4:11	4:35

Times are adjusted for Daylight Saving Time.

2016

JANUARY
S	M	T	W	T	F	S
					1	2
3	4	5	6	7	8	9
10	11	12	13	14	15	16
17	18	19	20	21	22	23
24	25	26	27	28	29	30
31						

FEBRUARY
S	M	T	W	T	F	S
	1	2	3	4	5	6
7	8	9	10	11	12	13
14	15	16	17	18	19	20
21	22	23	24	25	26	27
28	29					

MARCH
S	M	T	W	T	F	S
		1	2	3	4	5
6	7	8	9	10	11	12
13	14	15	16	17	18	19
20	21	22	23	24	25	26
27	28	29	30	31		

APRIL
S	M	T	W	T	F	S
					1	2
3	4	5	6	7	8	9
10	11	12	13	14	15	16
17	18	19	20	21	22	23
24	25	26	27	28	29	30

MAY
S	M	T	W	T	F	S
1	2	3	4	5	6	7
8	9	10	11	12	13	14
15	16	17	18	19	20	21
22	23	24	25	26	27	28
29	30	31				

JUNE
S	M	T	W	T	F	S
			1	2	3	4
5	6	7	8	9	10	11
12	13	14	15	16	17	18
19	20	21	22	23	24	25
26	27	28	29	30		

JULY
S	M	T	W	T	F	S
					1	2
3	4	5	6	7	8	9
10	11	12	13	14	15	16
17	18	19	20	21	22	23
24	25	26	27	28	29	30
31						

AUGUST
S	M	T	W	T	F	S
	1	2	3	4	5	6
7	8	9	10	11	12	13
14	15	16	17	18	19	20
21	22	23	24	25	26	27
28	29	30	31			

SEPTEMBER
S	M	T	W	T	F	S
				1	2	3
4	5	6	7	8	9	10
11	12	13	14	15	16	17
18	19	20	21	22	23	24
25	26	27	28	29	30	

OCTOBER
S	M	T	W	T	F	S
						1
2	3	4	5	6	7	8
9	10	11	12	13	14	15
16	17	18	19	20	21	22
23	24	25	26	27	28	29
30	31					

NOVEMBER
S	M	T	W	T	F	S
		1	2	3	4	5
6	7	8	9	10	11	12
13	14	15	16	17	18	19
20	21	22	23	24	25	26
27	28	29	30			

DECEMBER
S	M	T	W	T	F	S
				1	2	3
4	5	6	7	8	9	10
11	12	13	14	15	16	17
18	19	20	21	22	23	24
25	26	27	28	29	30	31

2017

JANUARY
S	M	T	W	T	F	S
1	2	3	4	5	6	7
8	9	10	11	12	13	14
15	16	17	18	19	20	21
22	23	24	25	26	27	28
29	30	31				

FEBRUARY
S	M	T	W	T	F	S
			1	2	3	4
5	6	7	8	9	10	11
12	13	14	15	16	17	18
19	20	21	22	23	24	25
26	27	28				

MARCH
S	M	T	W	T	F	S
			1	2	3	4
5	6	7	8	9	10	11
12	13	14	15	16	17	18
19	20	21	22	23	24	25
26	27	28	29	30	31	

APRIL
S	M	T	W	T	F	S
						1
2	3	4	5	6	7	8
9	10	11	12	13	14	15
16	17	18	19	20	21	22
23	24	25	26	27	28	29
30						

MAY
S	M	T	W	T	F	S
	1	2	3	4	5	6
7	8	9	10	11	12	13
14	15	16	17	18	19	20
21	22	23	24	25	26	27
28	29	30	31			

JUNE
S	M	T	W	T	F	S
				1	2	3
4	5	6	7	8	9	10
11	12	13	14	15	16	17
18	19	20	21	22	23	24
25	26	27	28	29	30	

JULY
S	M	T	W	T	F	S
						1
2	3	4	5	6	7	8
9	10	11	12	13	14	15
16	17	18	19	20	21	22
23	24	25	26	27	28	29
30	31					

AUGUST
S	M	T	W	T	F	S
		1	2	3	4	5
6	7	8	9	10	11	12
13	14	15	16	17	18	19
20	21	22	23	24	25	26
27	28	29	30	31		

SEPTEMBER
S	M	T	W	T	F	S
					1	2
3	4	5	6	7	8	9
10	11	12	13	14	15	16
17	18	19	20	21	22	23
24	25	26	27	28	29	30

OCTOBER
S	M	T	W	T	F	S
1	2	3	4	5	6	7
8	9	10	11	12	13	14
15	16	17	18	19	20	21
22	23	24	25	26	27	28
29	30	31				

NOVEMBER
S	M	T	W	T	F	S
			1	2	3	4
5	6	7	8	9	10	11
12	13	14	15	16	17	18
19	20	21	22	23	24	25
26	27	28	29	30		

DECEMBER
S	M	T	W	T	F	S
					1	2
3	4	5	6	7	8	9
10	11	12	13	14	15	16
17	18	19	20	21	22	23
24	25	26	27	28	29	30
31						